GRIMMY™
Inc.

Always Stop and Smell the Hydrants

by Mike Peters

TOR®

A TOM DOHERTY ASSOCIATES BOOK
NEW YORK

This is a work of fiction. All the characters and events portrayed in this book are either products of the author's imagination or are used fictitiously.

GRIMMY™: ALWAYS STOP AND SMELL THE HYDRANTS

This book contains material published previously in a trade edition as *Grimmy: The Postman Always Screams Twice.*

A Tor Book
Published by Tom Doherty Associates, Inc.
175 Fifth Avenue
New York, NY 10010

Tor Books on the World Wide Web:
http://www.tor.com

Tor® is a registered trademark of Tom Doherty Associates, Inc.

ISBN: 0-812-59091-0

First edition: February 1996
First mass market edition: April 1999

Printed in the United States of America

0 9 8 7 6 5 4 3 2 1

PAY TOILET? GREAT.. NOW HOW AM I SUPPOSED TO GET A DRINK?
ACME PAY TOILET
EVERYBODY, LIMBO...
ACME PAY TOILET
7-1

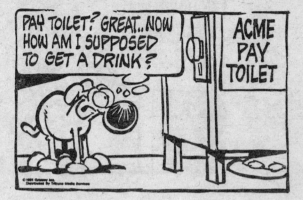

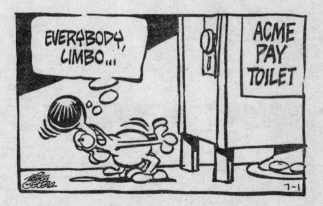

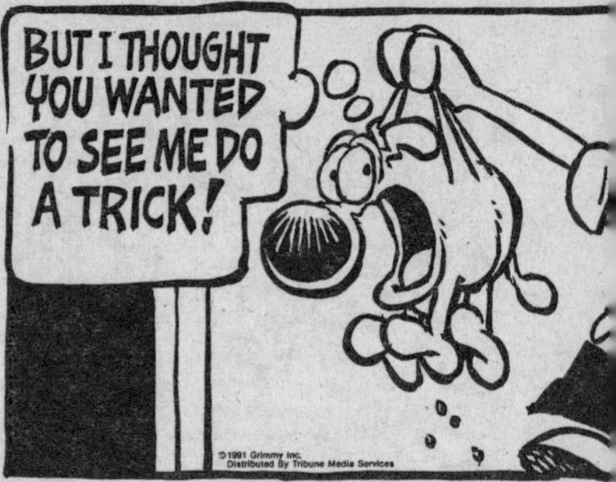
BUT I THOUGHT YOU WANTED TO SEE ME DO A TRICK!
©1991 Grimmy Inc.
Distributed By Tribune Media Services

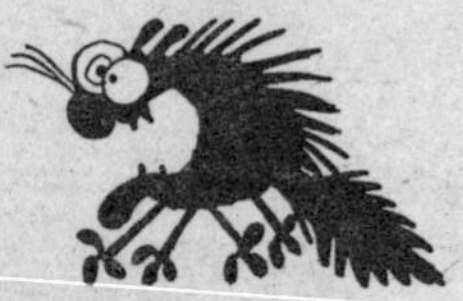

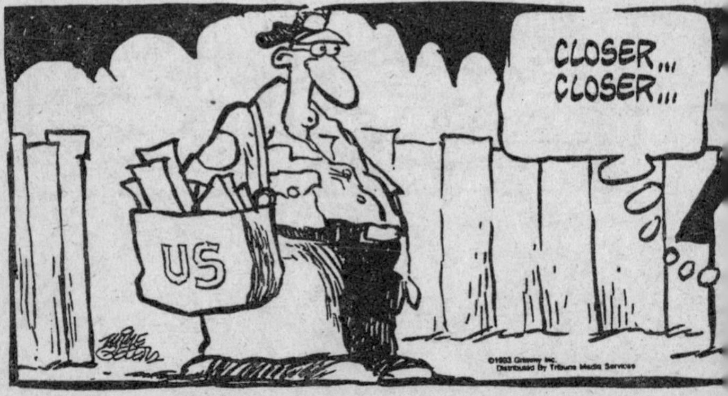
CLOSER... CLOSER...
US
Grimmy Inc.
Distributed By Tribune Media Services

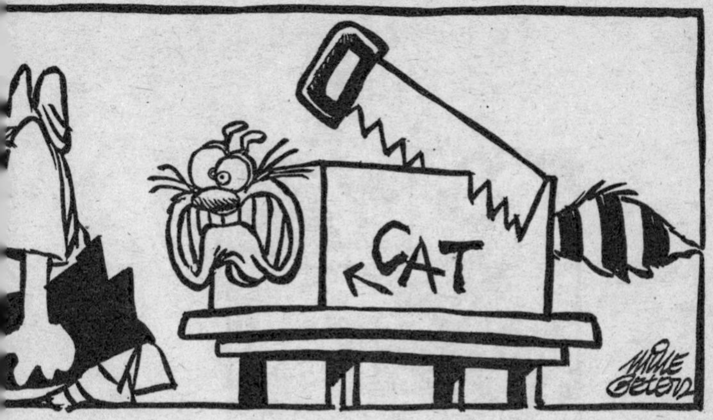
CAT
Mike Peters

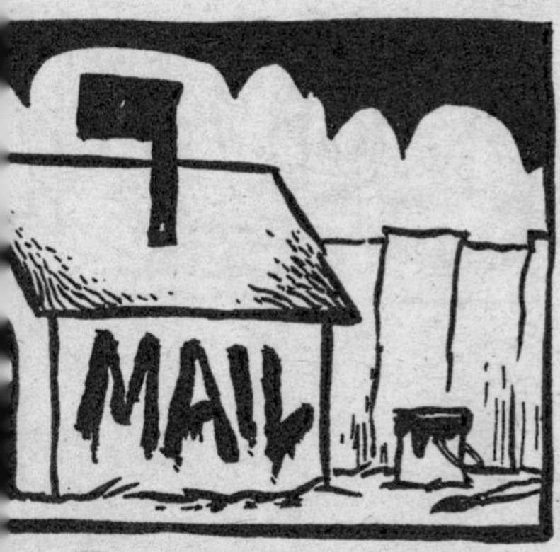
MAIL

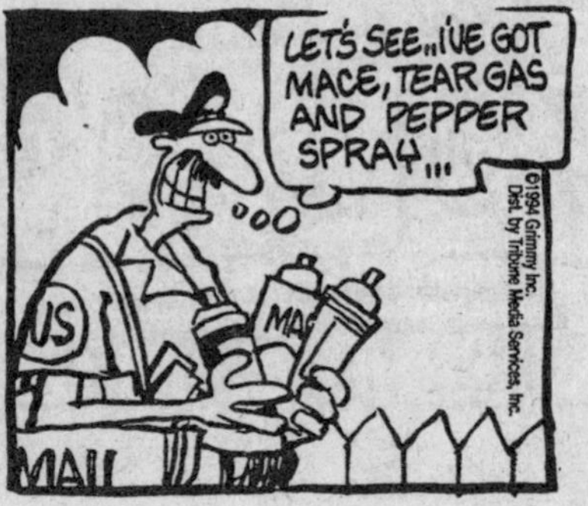
LET'S SEE... I'VE GOT MACE, TEAR GAS AND PEPPER SPRAY...
©1994 Grimmy Inc.
Dist. by Tribune Media Services, Inc.
US
MAC
MAIL

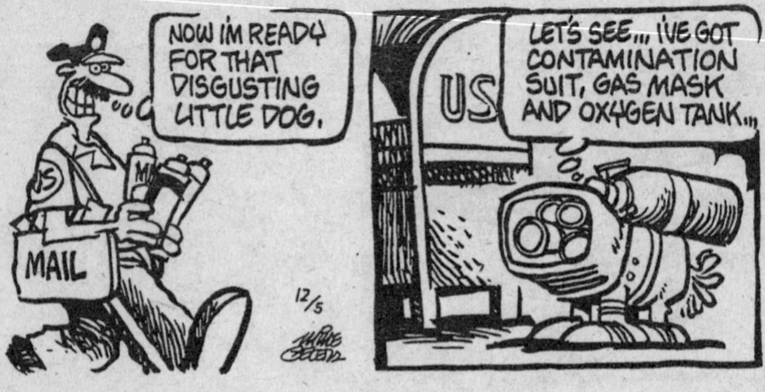
NOW I'M READY FOR THAT DISGUSTING LITTLE DOG.
US
MAIL
12/5
LET'S SEE... I'VE GOT CONTAMINATION SUIT, GAS MASK AND OXYGEN TANK...
US

I KNOW HE'S GOING TO JUMP OUT AND SCARE ME WHEN I OPEN THIS MAILBOX.
AIL
12/6
I KNOW IT... I KNOW HE'S GOING TO SCARE ME. I KNOW IT! I KNOW IT!
©1994 Grimmy Inc.
Dist. by Tribune Media Services, Inc.
WHEW...
...I LUCKED OUT THAT TIME.
MAIL

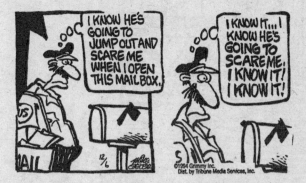

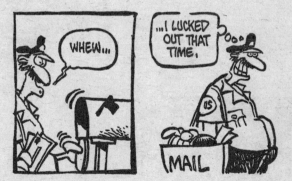

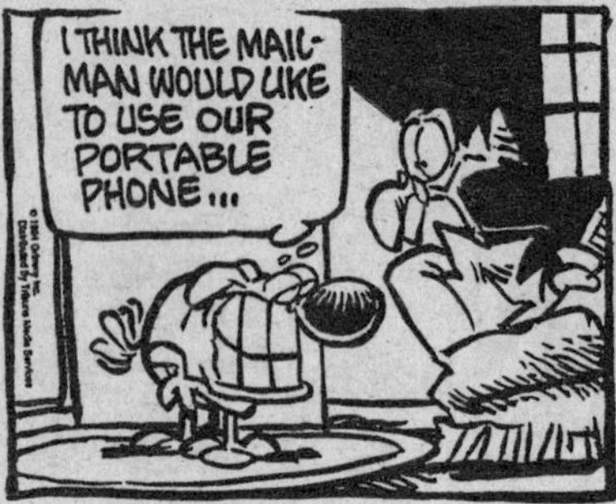
I THINK THE MAILMAN WOULD LIKE TO USE OUR PORTABLE PHONE...

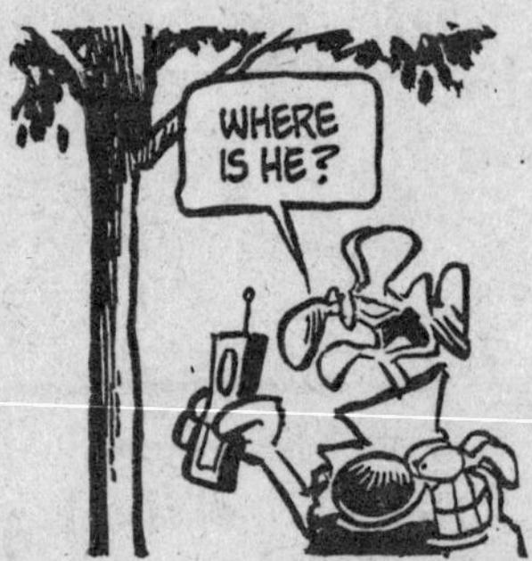
WHERE IS HE?

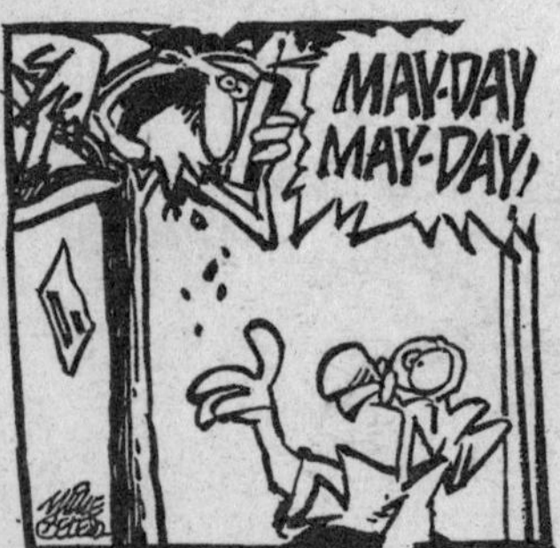
MAY-DAY MAY-DAY!

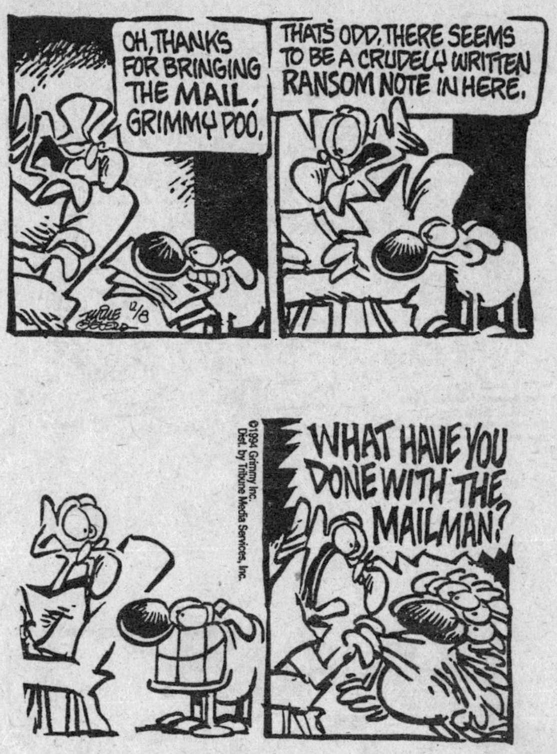
OH, THANKS FOR BRINGING THE MAIL, GRIMMY POO.
THAT'S ODD, THERE SEEMS TO BE A CRUDELY WRITTEN RANSOM NOTE IN HERE.
WHAT HAVE YOU DONE WITH THE MAILMAN?
©1994 Grimmy Inc.
Dist. by Tribune Media Services, Inc.

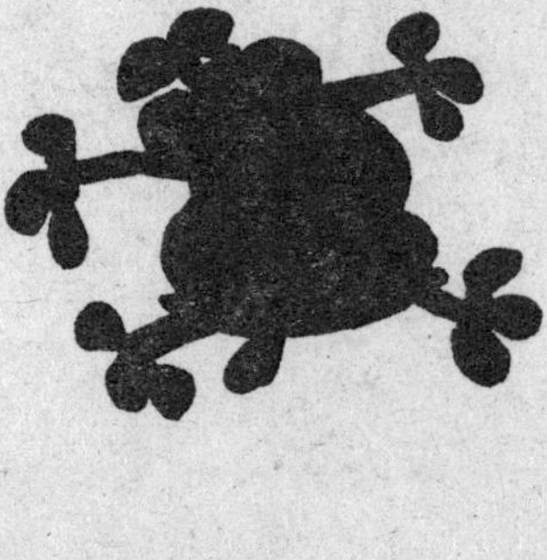

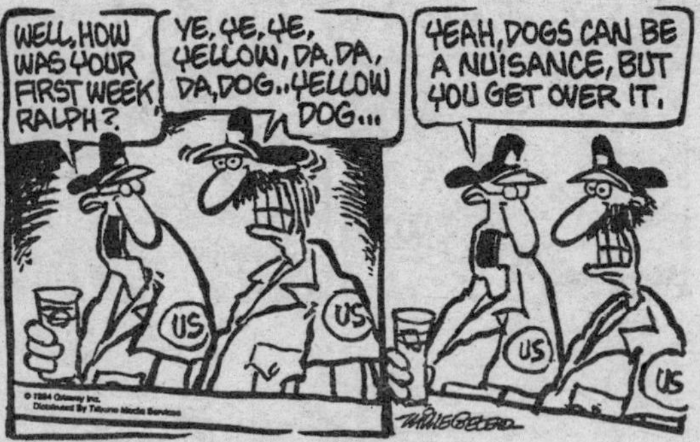
WELL, HOW WAS YOUR FIRST WEEK, RALPH?
YE, YE, YE, YELLOW, DA, DA, DA, DOG.. YELLOW DOG...
YEAH, DOGS CAN BE A NUISANCE, BUT YOU GET OVER IT.

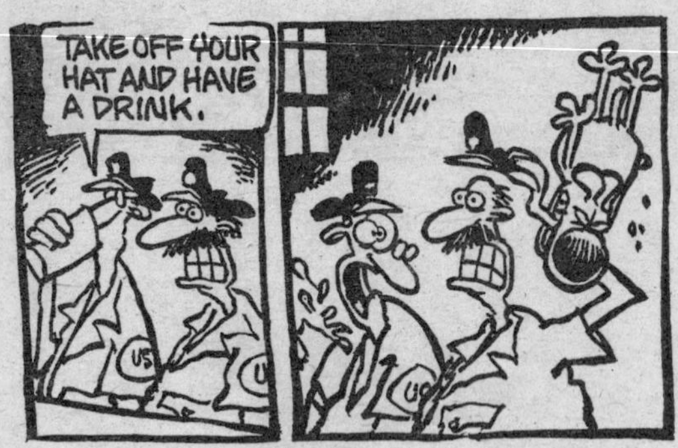
TAKE OFF YOUR HAT AND HAVE A DRINK.

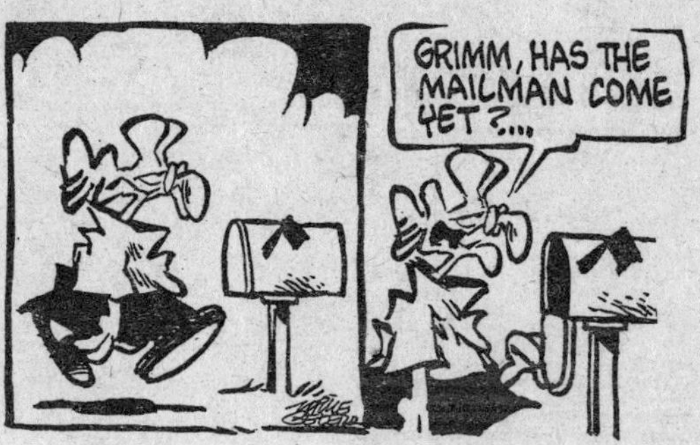
GRIMM, HAS THE MAILMAN COME YET?...

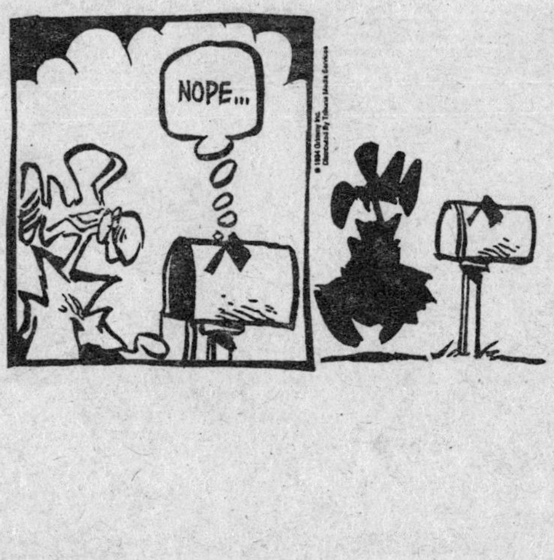
NOPE...

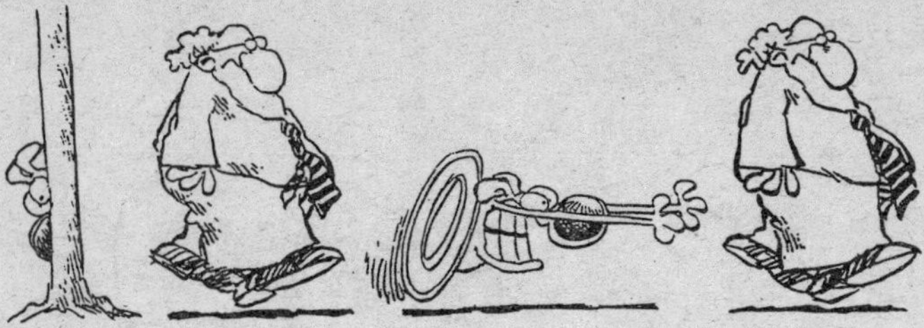

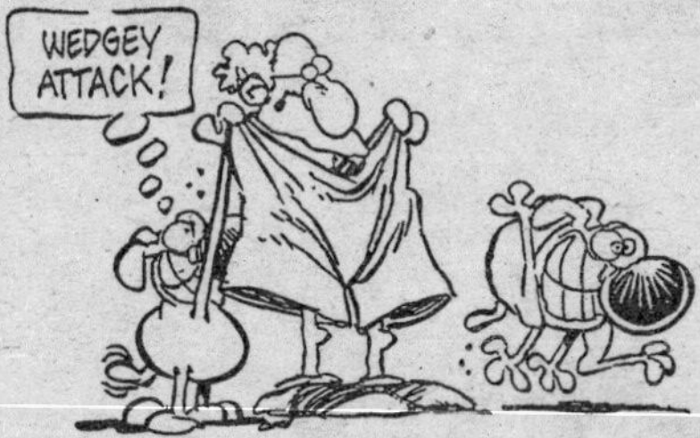
WEDGEY ATTACK!

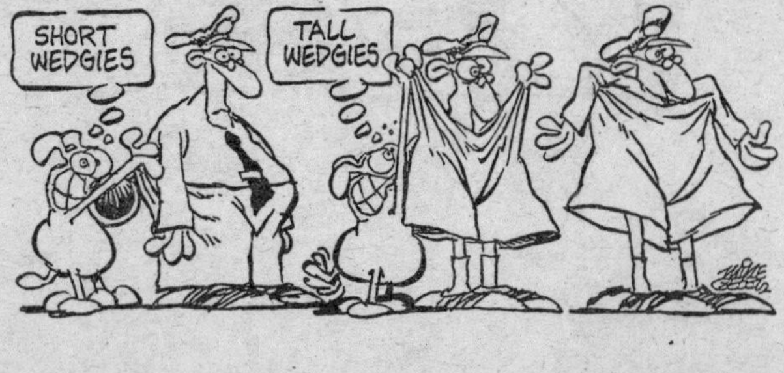
SHORT WEDGIES
TALL WEDGIES

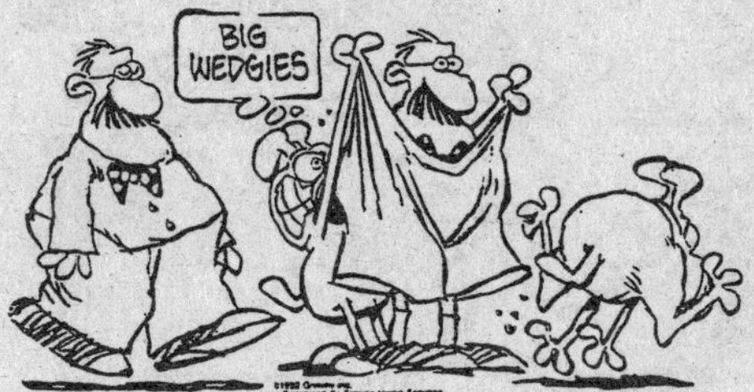
BIG WEDGIES

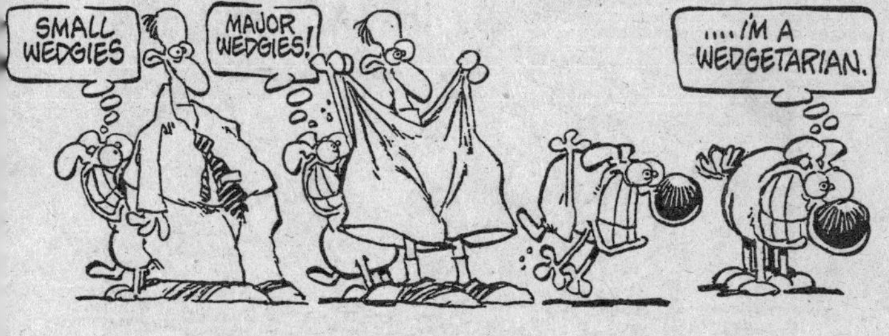
SMALL WEDGIES
MAJOR WEDGIES!
....I'M A WEDGETARIAN.

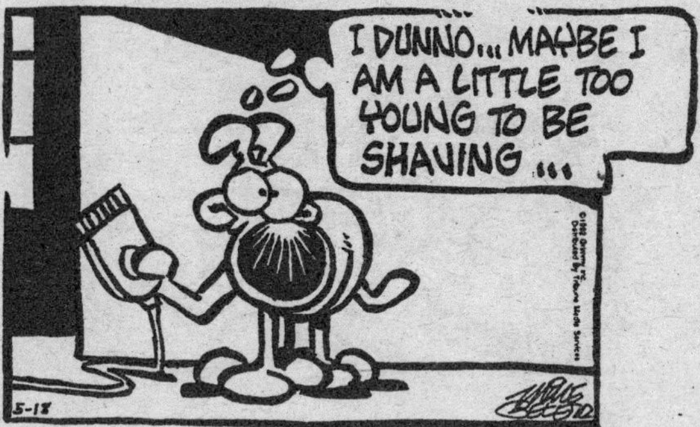
I DUNNO... MAYBE I AM A LITTLE TOO YOUNG TO BE SHAVING...
5-18

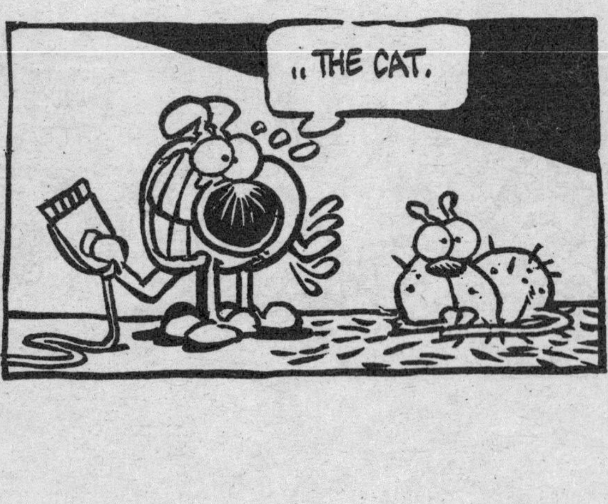
.. THE CAT.

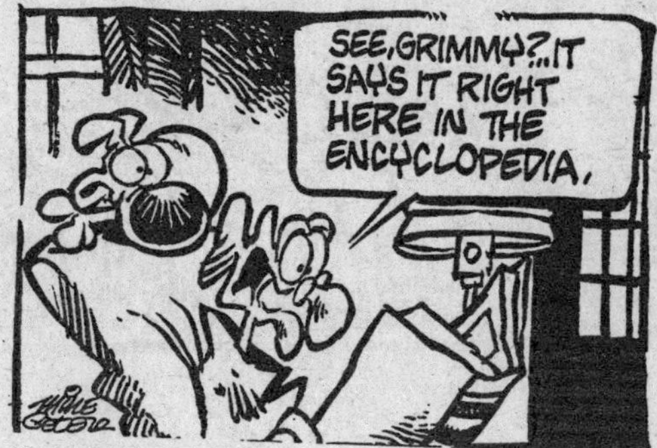
SEE, GRIMMY?...IT SAYS IT RIGHT HERE IN THE ENCYCLOPEDIA.

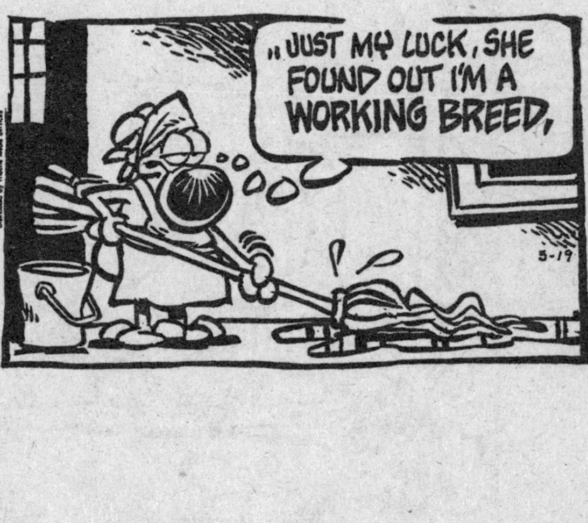
..JUST MY LUCK, SHE FOUND OUT I'M A WORKING BREED.
5-19

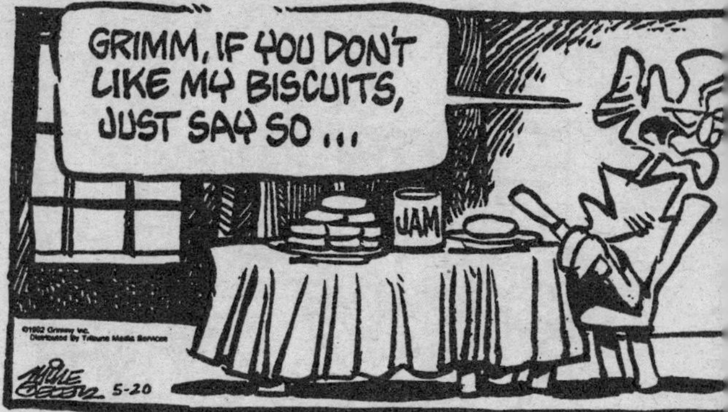
GRIMM, IF YOU DON'T LIKE MY BISCUITS, JUST SAY SO ...
JAM
5-20

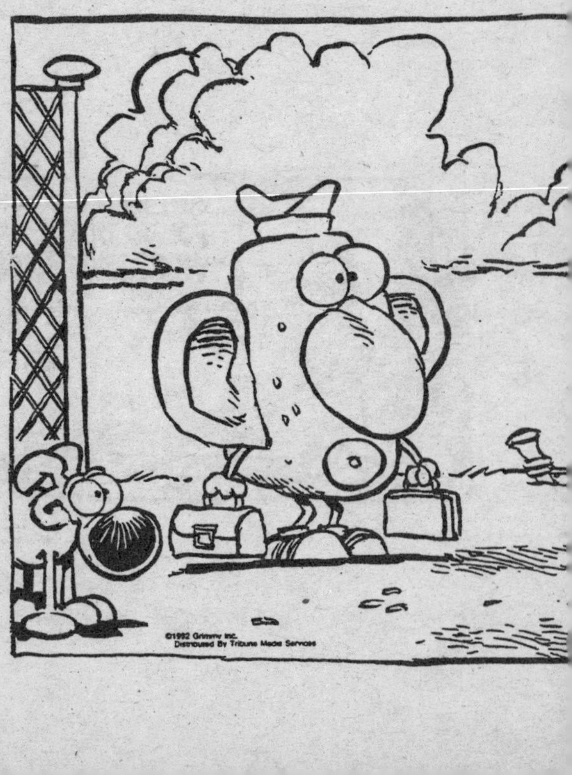
©1992 Grimmy Inc.
Distributed By Tribune Media Services

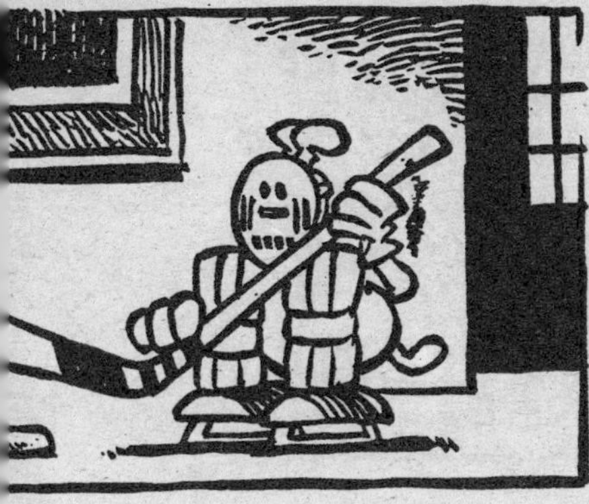

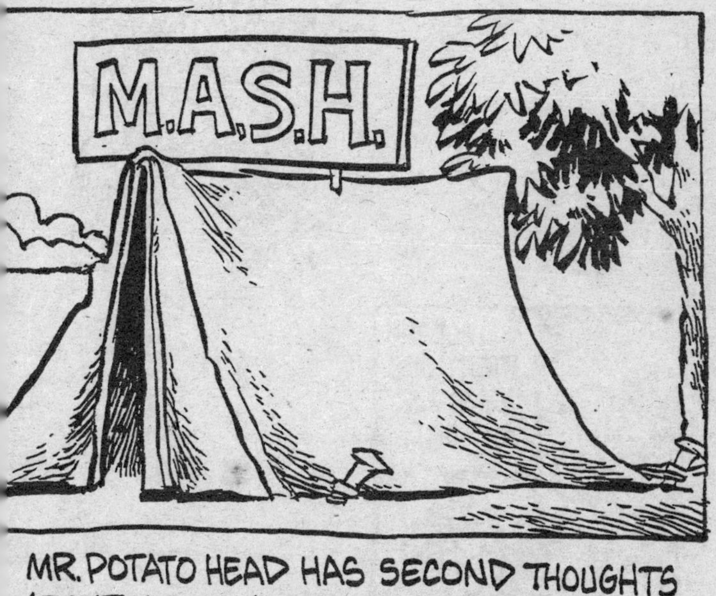
M.A.S.H.

MR. POTATO HEAD HAS SECOND THOUGHTS ABOUT HIS NEW MILITARY ASSIGNMENT.

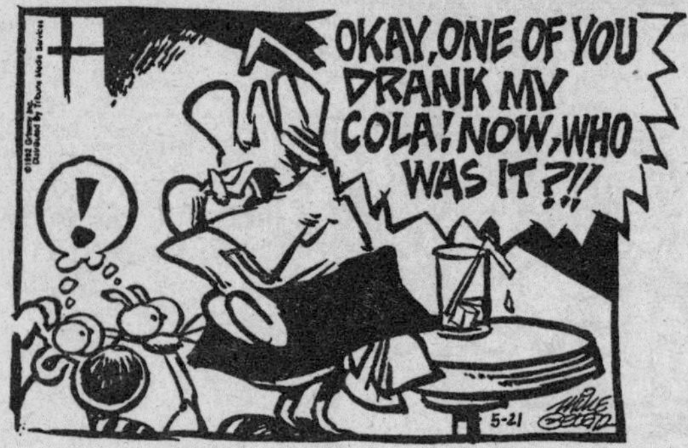
OKAY, ONE OF YOU DRANK MY COLA! NOW, WHO WAS IT?!!
!
5-21

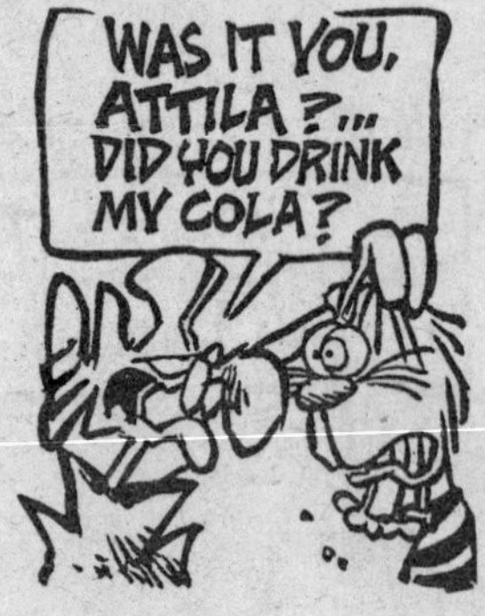
WAS IT YOU, ATTILA?... DID YOU DRINK MY COLA?

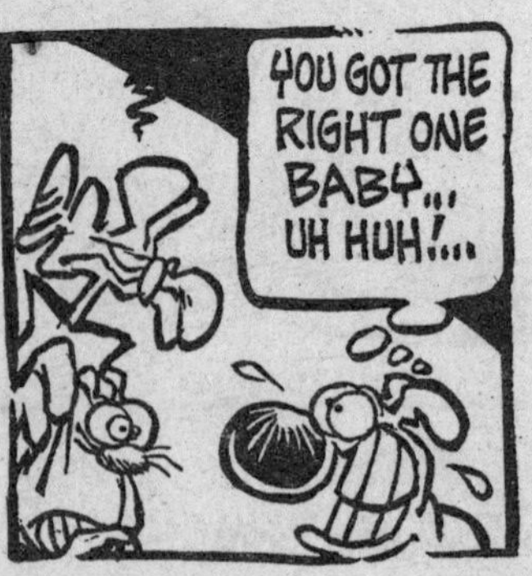
YOU GOT THE RIGHT ONE BABY... UH HUH!...

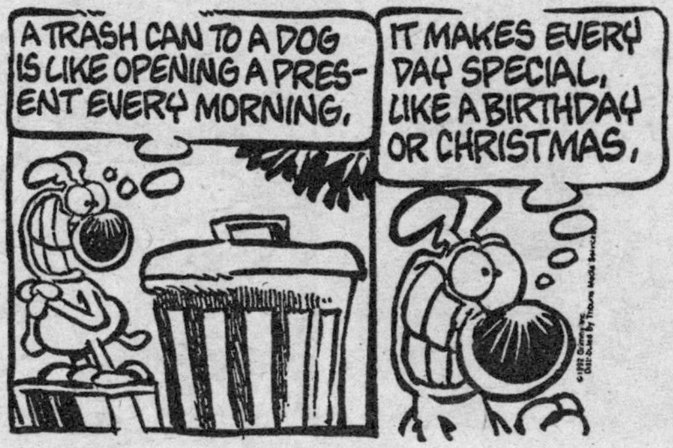

A TRASH CAN TO A DOG IS LIKE OPENING A PRES-ENT EVERY MORNING.
IT MAKES EVERY DAY SPECIAL, LIKE A BIRTHDAY OR CHRISTMAS.

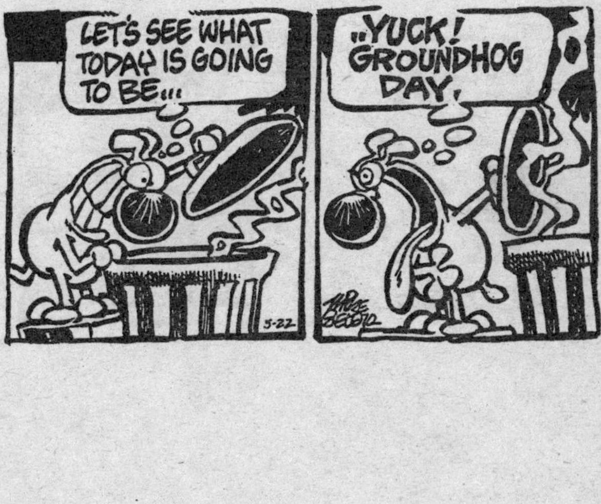

LET'S SEE WHAT TODAY IS GOING TO BE...
5-22
..YUCK! GROUNDHOG DAY.

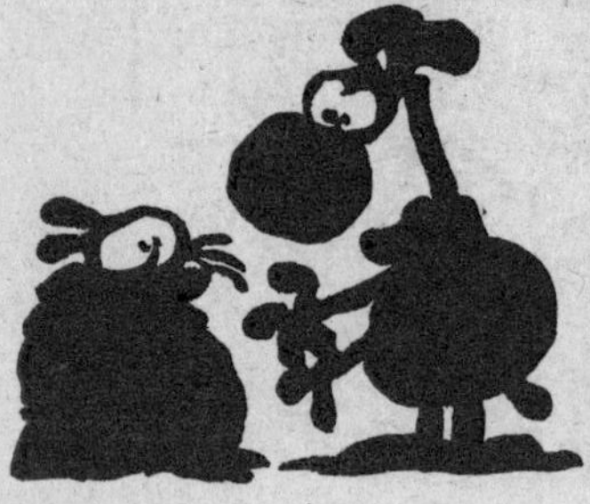

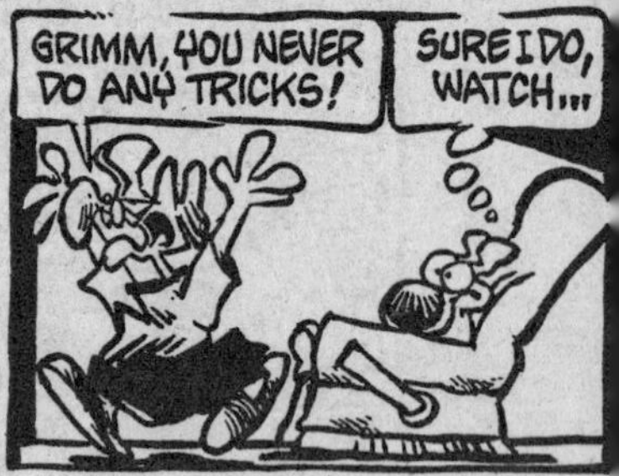
GRIMM, YOU NEVER DO ANY TRICKS!
SURE I DO, WATCH...

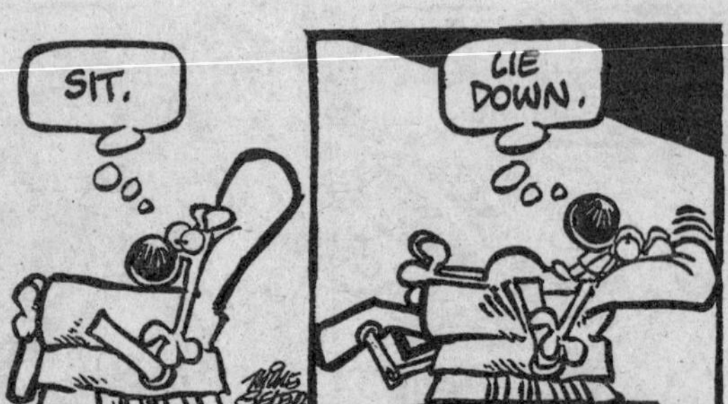
SIT.
LIE DOWN.

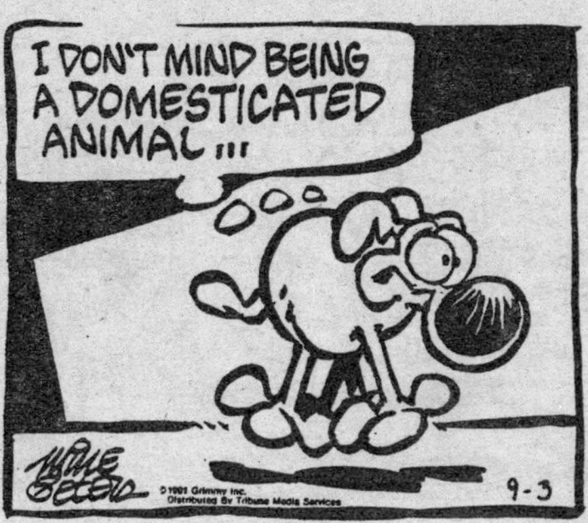
I DON'T MIND BEING A DOMESTICATED ANIMAL...
©1981 Grimmy Inc.
Distributed By Tribune Media Services
9-3

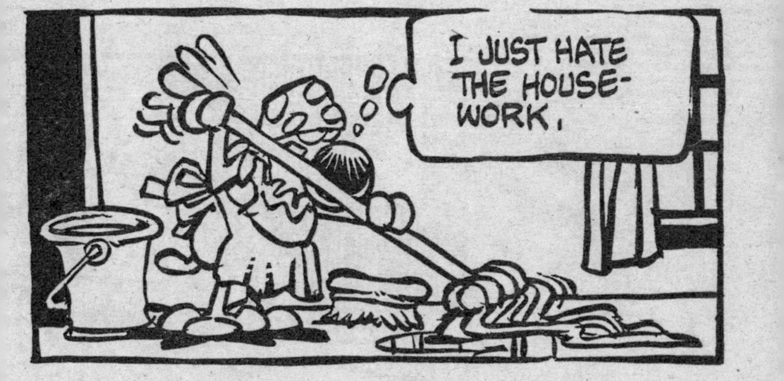
I JUST HATE THE HOUSE-WORK.

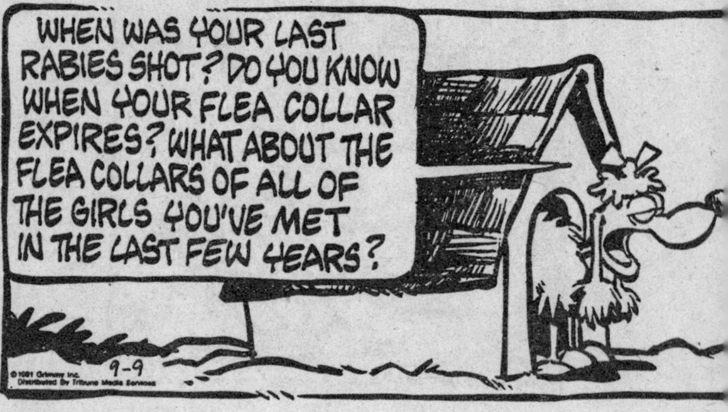
WHEN WAS YOUR LAST RABIES SHOT? DO YOU KNOW WHEN YOUR FLEA COLLAR EXPIRES? WHAT ABOUT THE FLEA COLLARS OF ALL OF THE GIRLS YOU'VE MET IN THE LAST FEW YEARS?
9-9
© 1981 Grimmy Inc.
Distributed By Tribune Media Services

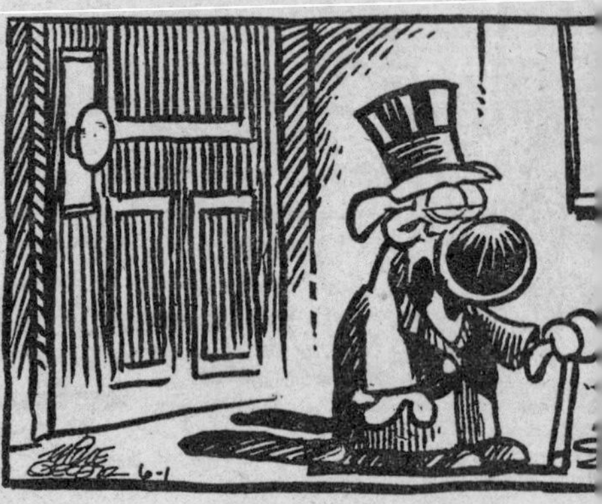
6-1

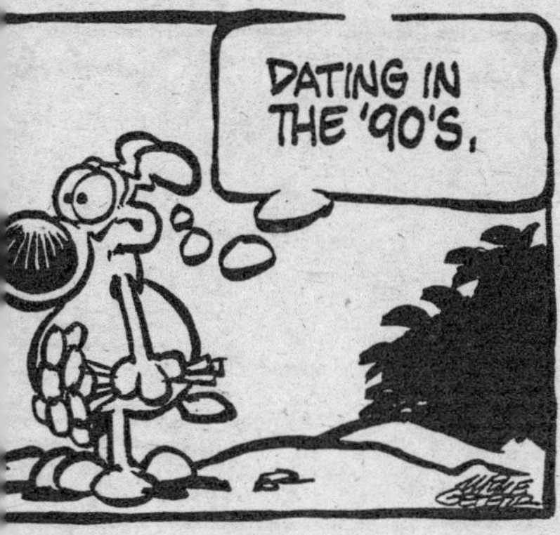
DATING IN
THE '90'S.

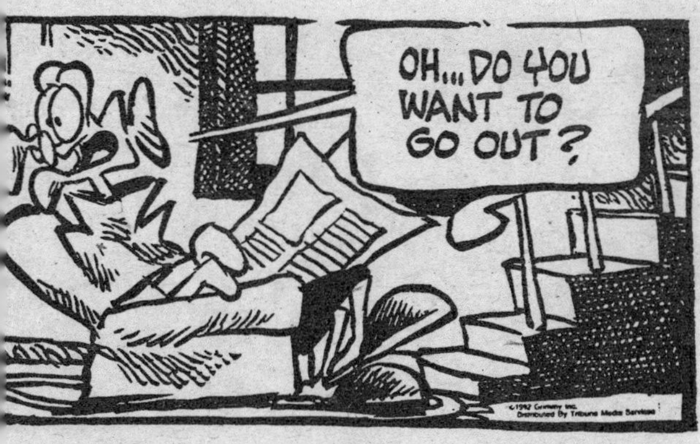
OH...DO YOU
WANT TO
GO OUT?

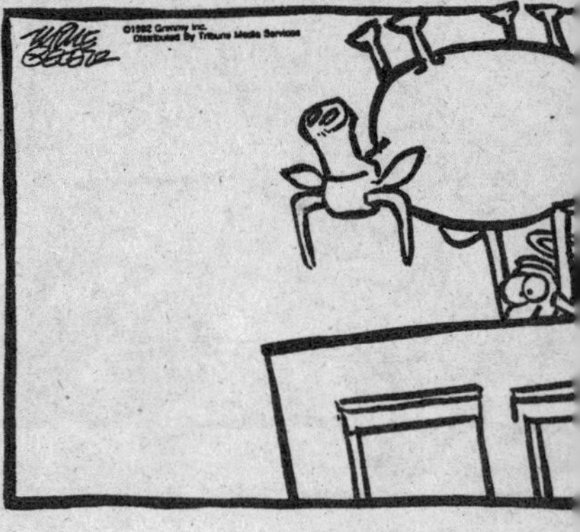
©1992 Grimmy Inc.
Distributed By Tribune Media Services

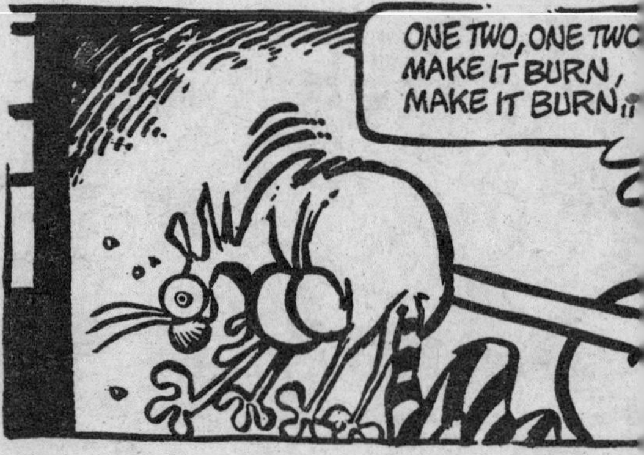
ONE TWO, ONE TWO
MAKE IT BURN,
MAKE IT BURN!!

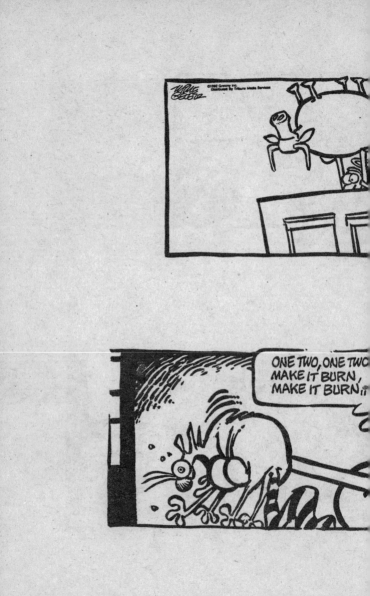

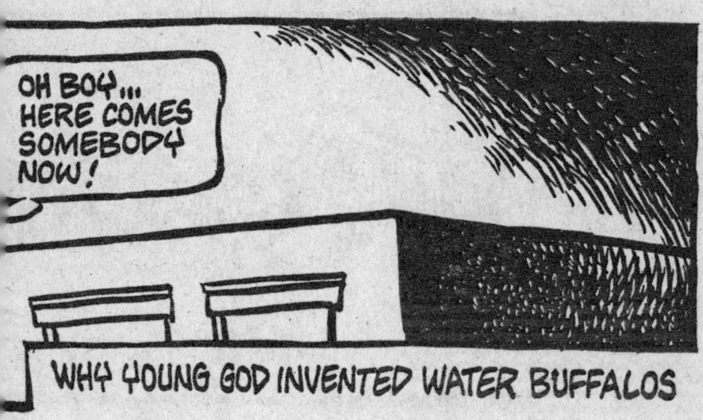
OH BOY... HERE COMES SOMEBODY NOW!
WHY YOUNG GOD INVENTED WATER BUFFALOS

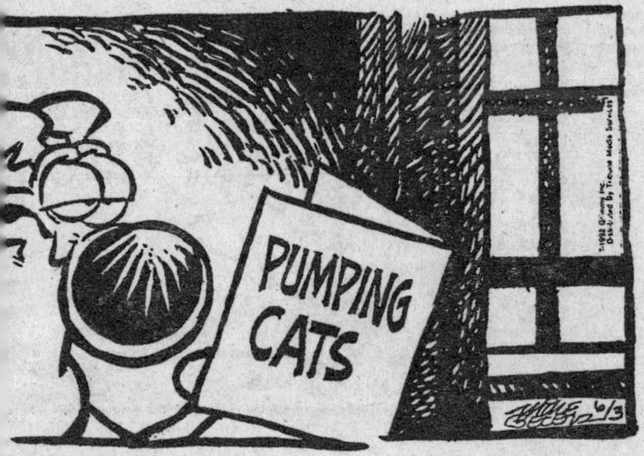
PUMPING CATS

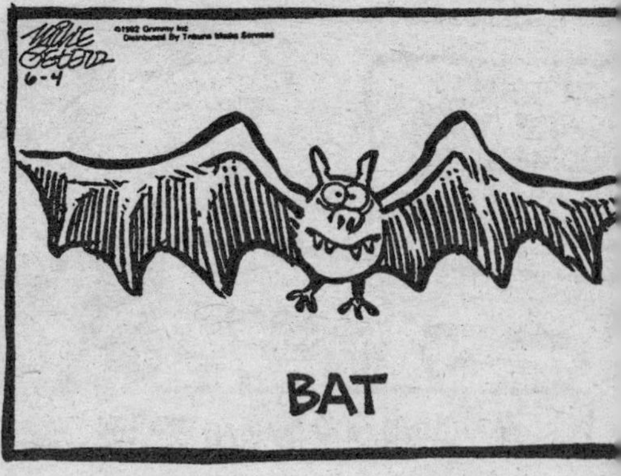

©1992 Grimmy Inc
Distributed By Tribune Media Services
6-4
BAT

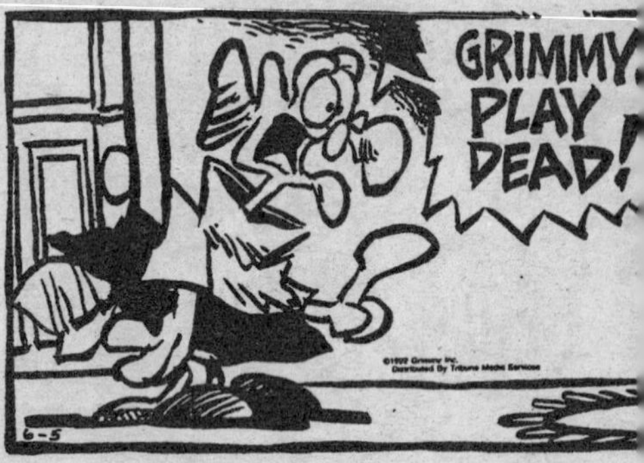

GRIMMY, PLAY DEAD!
©1992 Grimmy Inc.
Distributed By Tribune Media Services
6-5

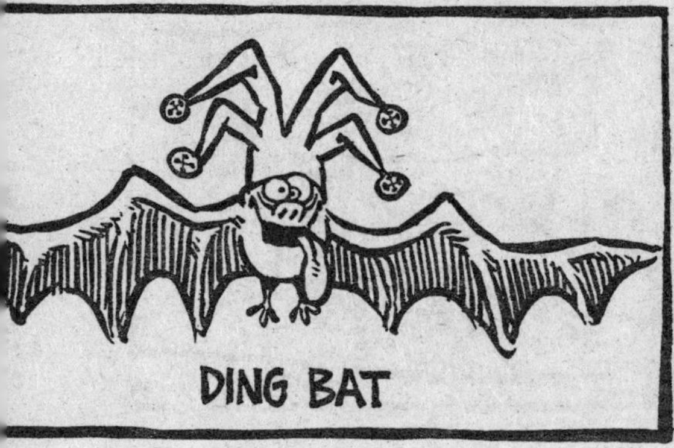
DING BAT

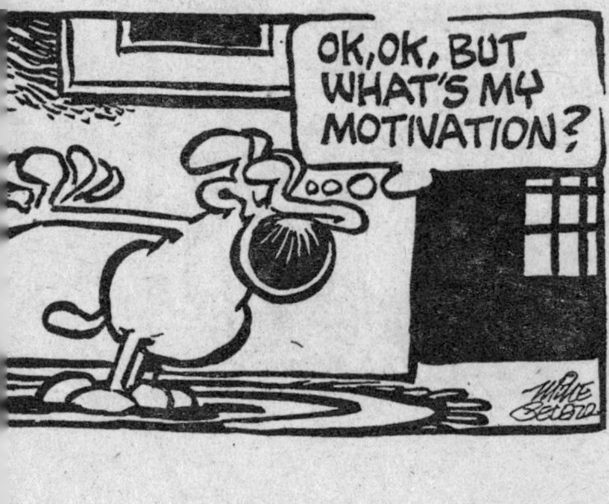
OK, OK, BUT WHAT'S MY MOTIVATION?

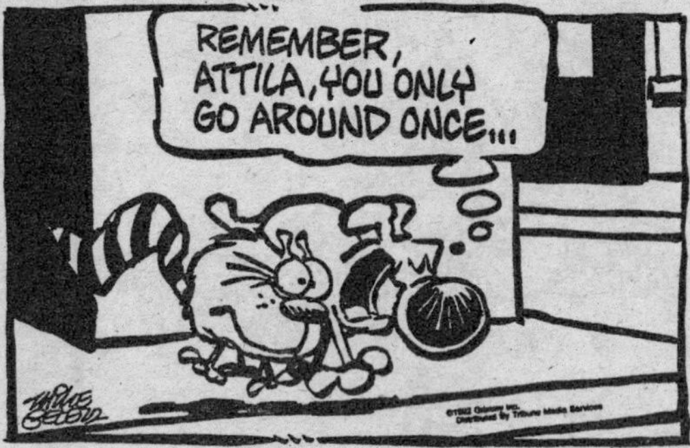
REMEMBER, ATTILA, YOU ONLY GO AROUND ONCE...

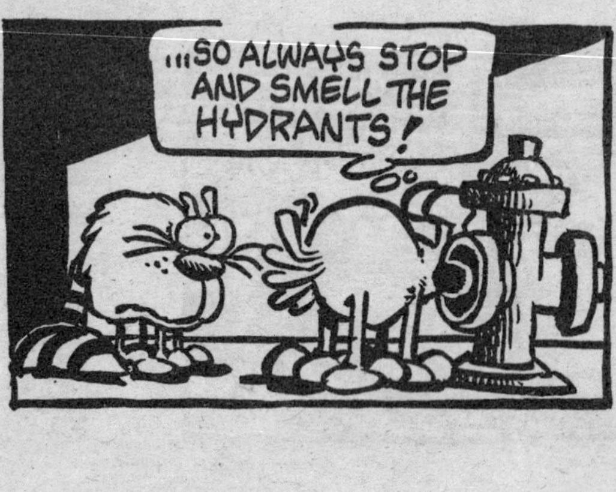
...SO ALWAYS STOP AND SMELL THE HYDRANTS!

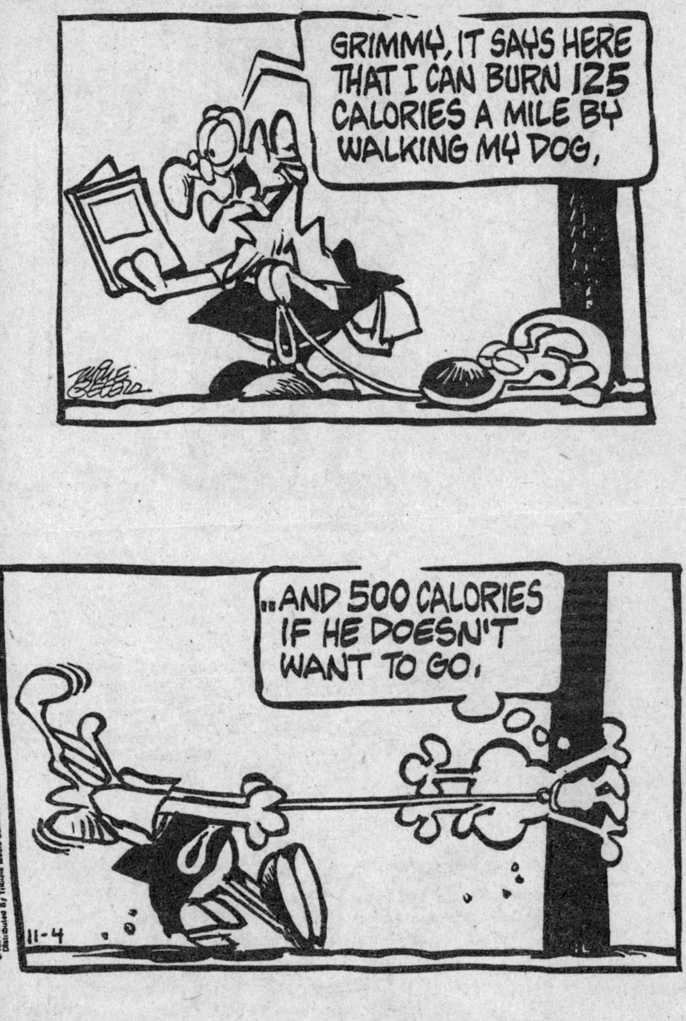
GRIMMY, IT SAYS HERE THAT I CAN BURN 125 CALORIES A MILE BY WALKING MY DOG,
..AND 500 CALORIES IF HE DOESN'T WANT TO GO.
11-4

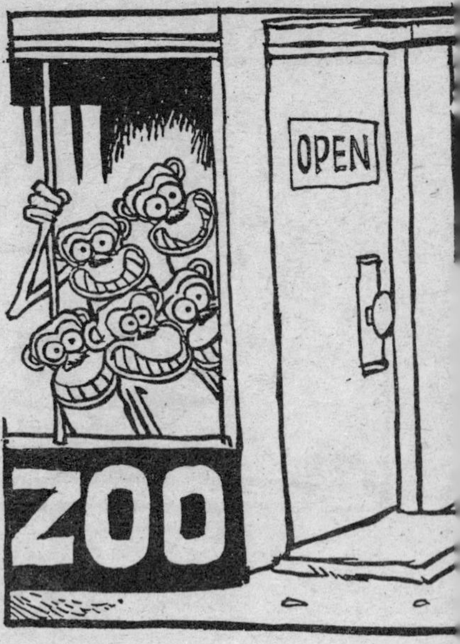
OPEN
ZOO

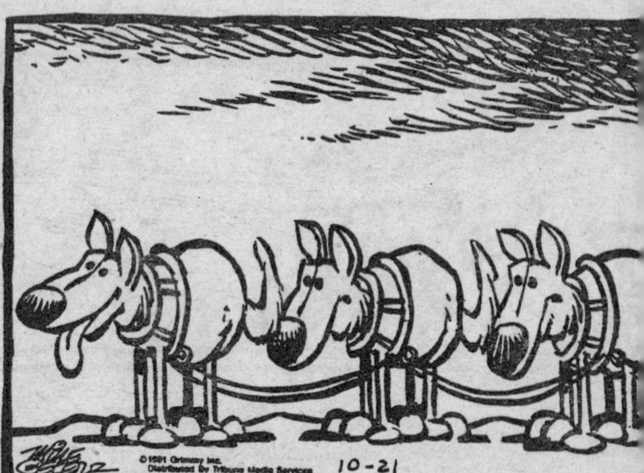
©1991 Grimmy Inc.
Distributed by Tribune Media Services
10-21

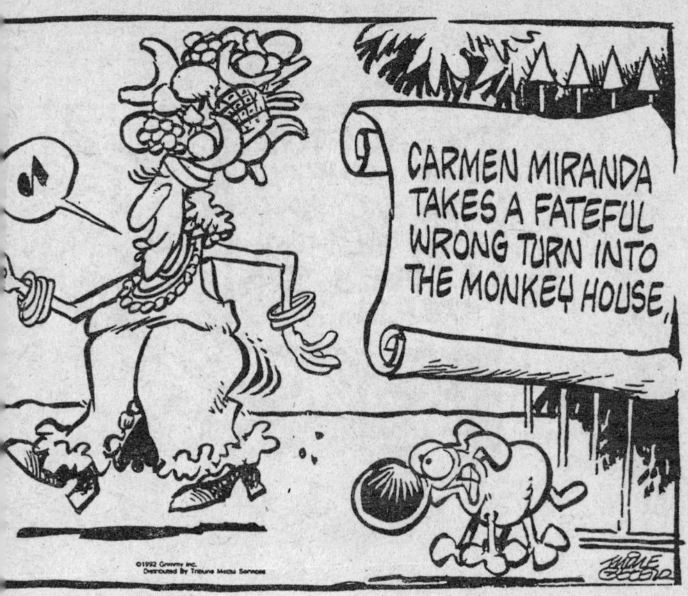
CARMEN MIRANDA TAKES A FATEFUL WRONG TURN INTO THE MONKEY HOUSE.
©1992 Grimmy Inc.
Distributed By Tribune Media Services

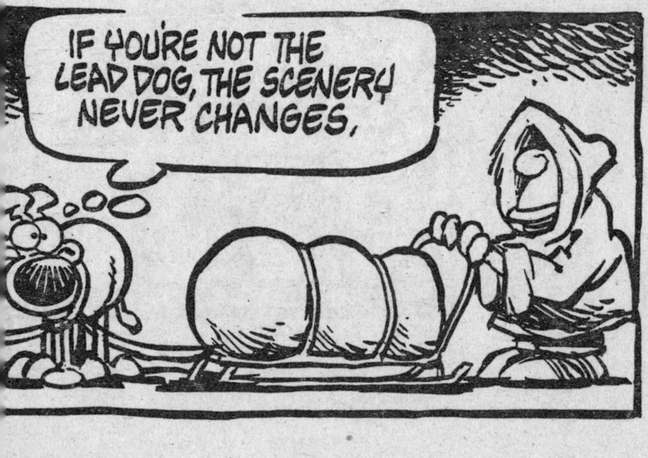
IF YOU'RE NOT THE LEAD DOG, THE SCENERY NEVER CHANGES.

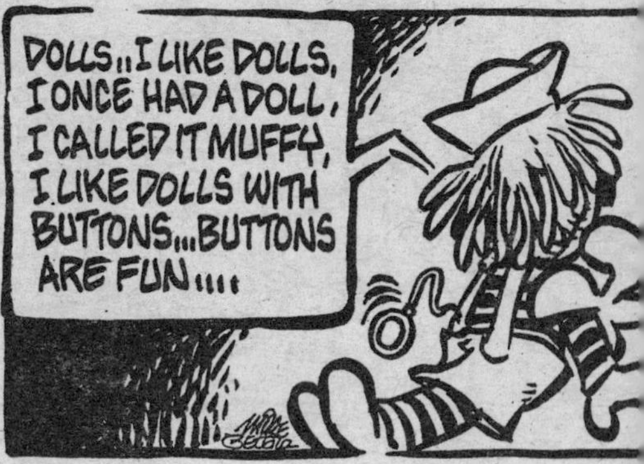
DOLLS..I LIKE DOLLS. I ONCE HAD A DOLL, I CALLED IT MUFFY, I LIKE DOLLS WITH BUTTONS...BUTTONS ARE FUN....

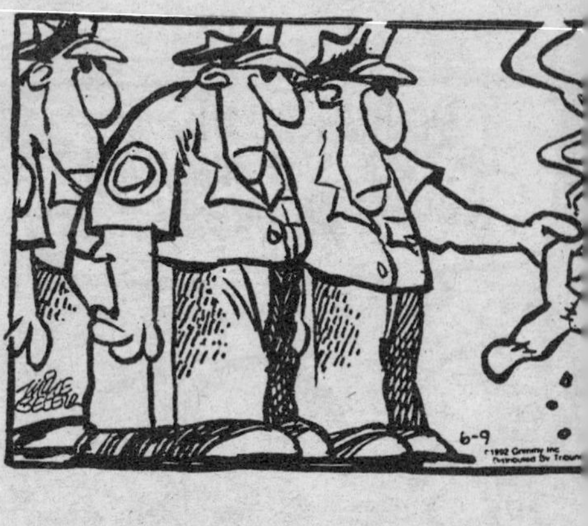
6-9

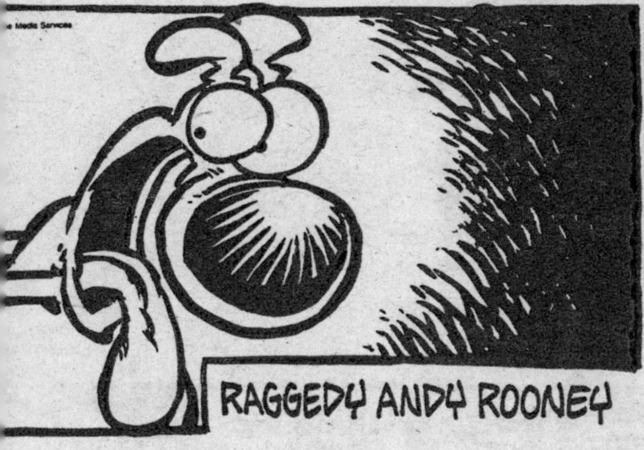
RAGGEDY ANDY ROONEY

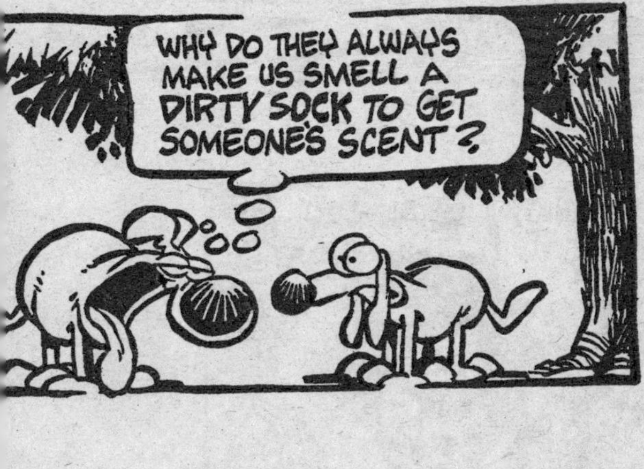
WHY DO THEY ALWAYS MAKE US SMELL A DIRTY SOCK TO GET SOMEONE'S SCENT?

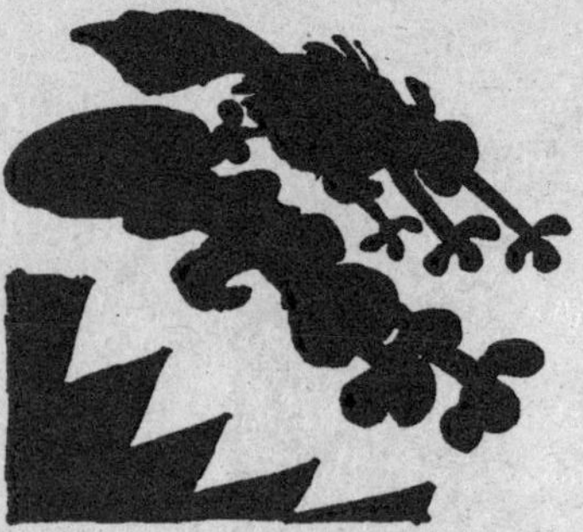

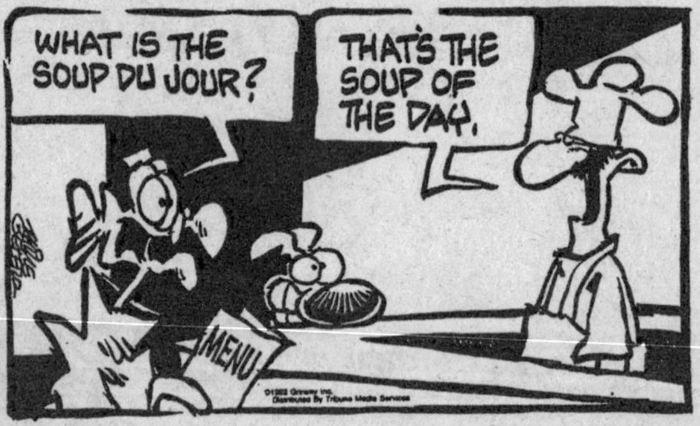
WHAT IS THE SOUP DU JOUR?
THAT'S THE SOUP OF THE DAY.
MENU
Grimmy Inc.
Distributed By Tribune Media Services

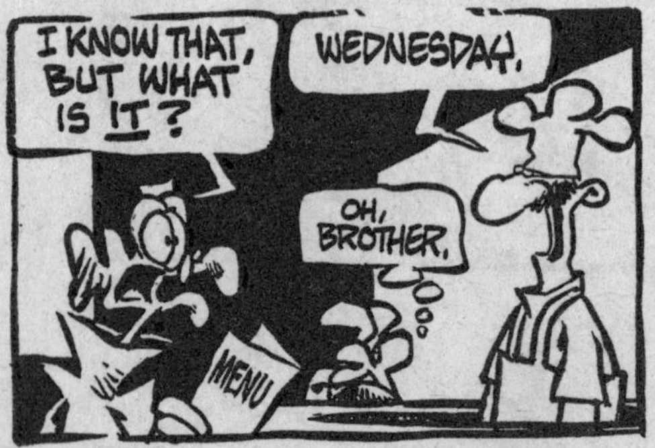
I KNOW THAT, BUT WHAT IS IT?
WEDNESDAY.
OH, BROTHER.
MENU

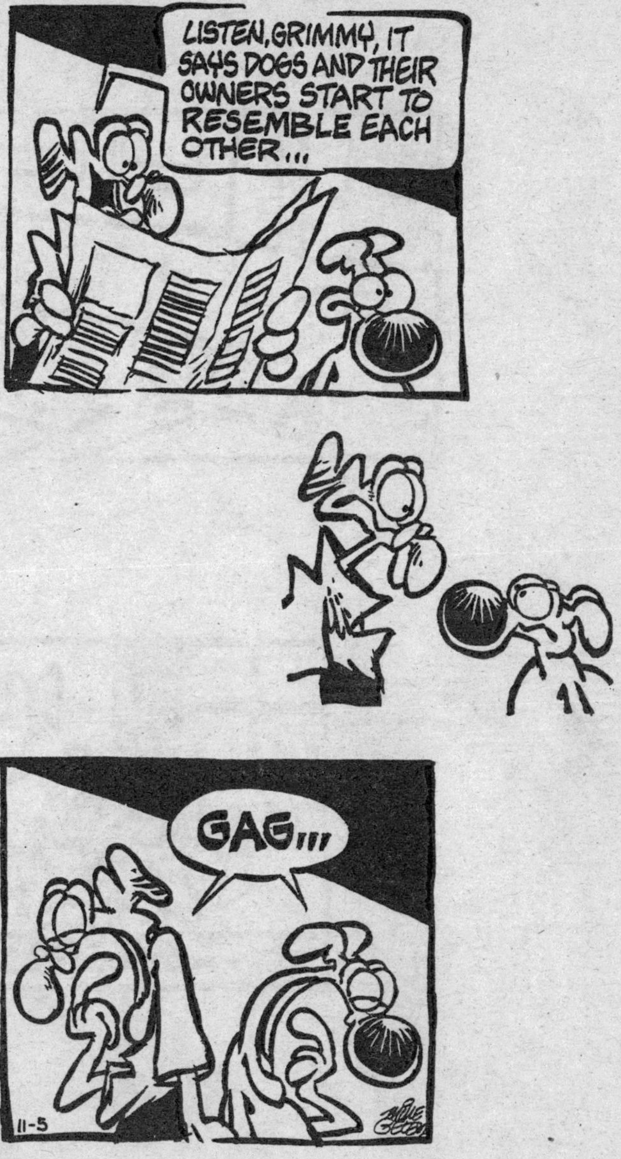

LISTEN, GRIMMY, IT SAYS DOGS AND THEIR OWNERS START TO RESEMBLE EACH OTHER...
GAG...
11-5
MIKE PETERS

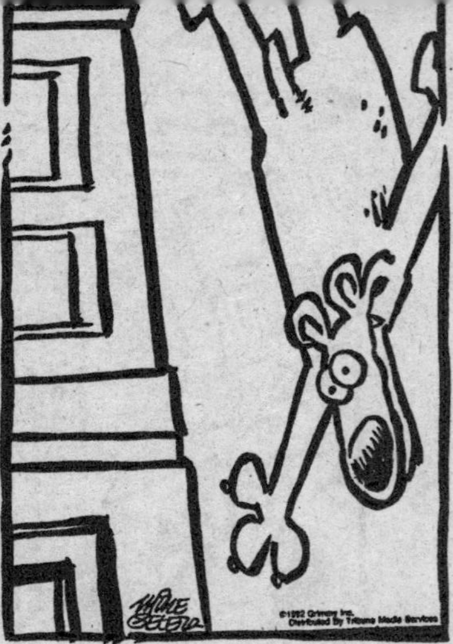
©1992 Grimmy Inc.
Distributed by Tribune Media Services

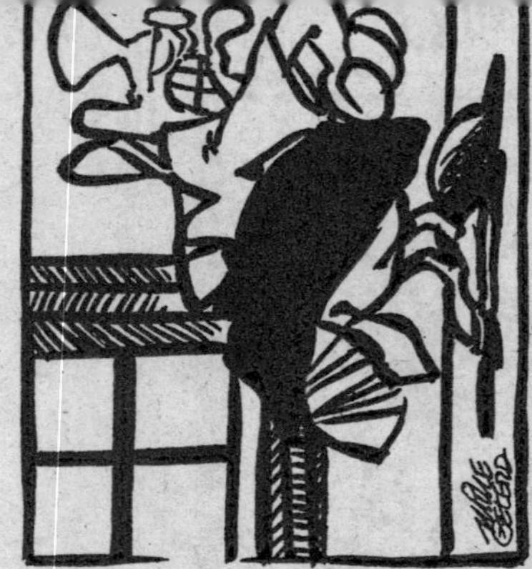

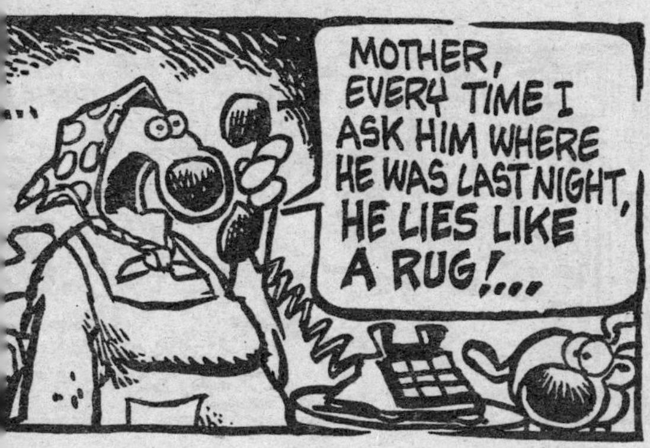
MOTHER, EVERY TIME I ASK HIM WHERE HE WAS LAST NIGHT, HE LIES LIKE A RUG!...

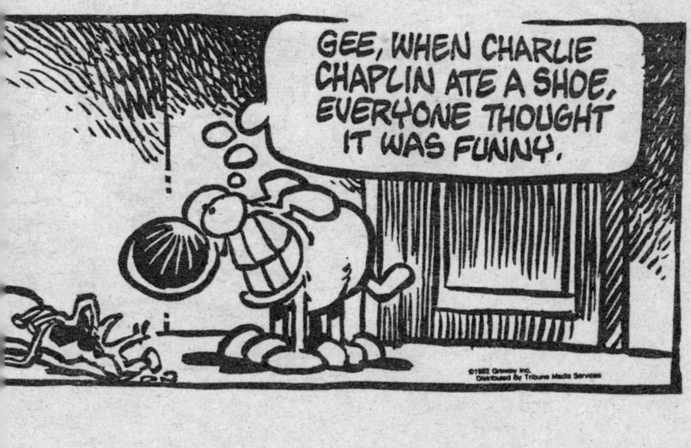
GEE, WHEN CHARLIE CHAPLIN ATE A SHOE, EVERYONE THOUGHT IT WAS FUNNY.
Distributed By Tribune Media Services

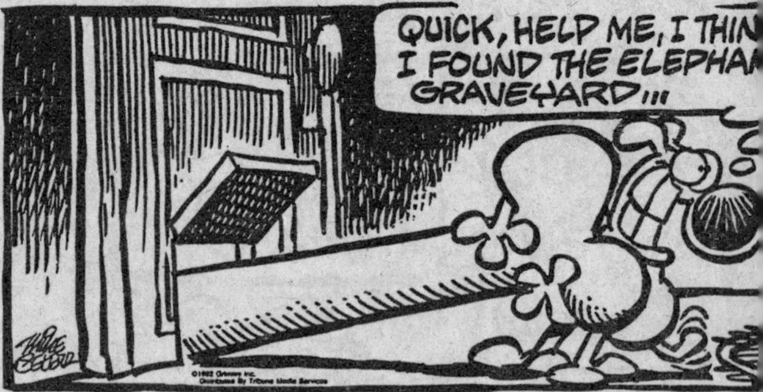
QUICK, HELP ME, I THIN
I FOUND THE ELEPHA
GRAVEYARD!!!

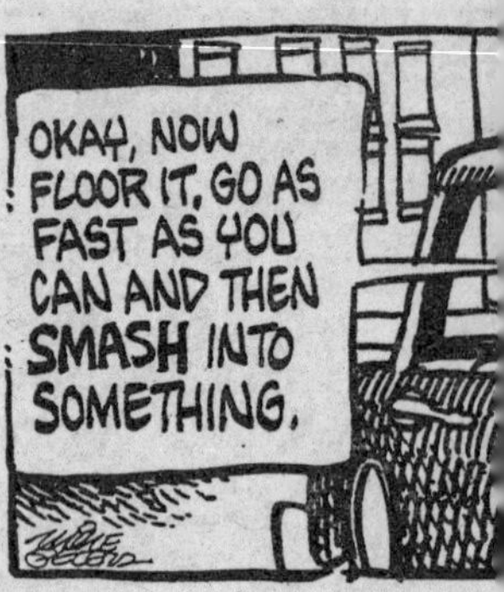
OKAY, NOW FLOOR IT, GO AS FAST AS YOU CAN AND THEN SMASH INTO SOMETHING.

GEE, I HOPE I DON'T SCREW UP THIS TIME.

CRASH DUMMY DRIVERS' SCHOOL

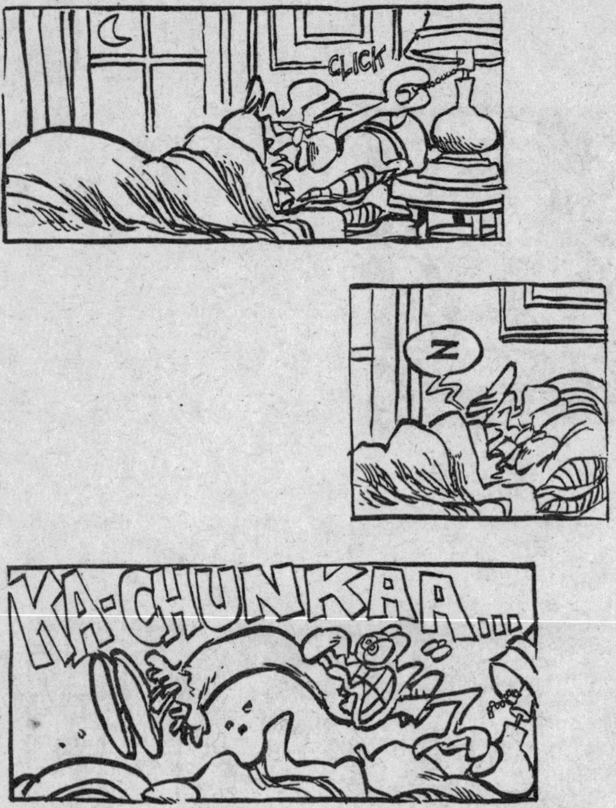
CLICK
Z
KA-CHUNKAA...
CHINKA CHINKA
CHINKACHINK

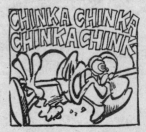

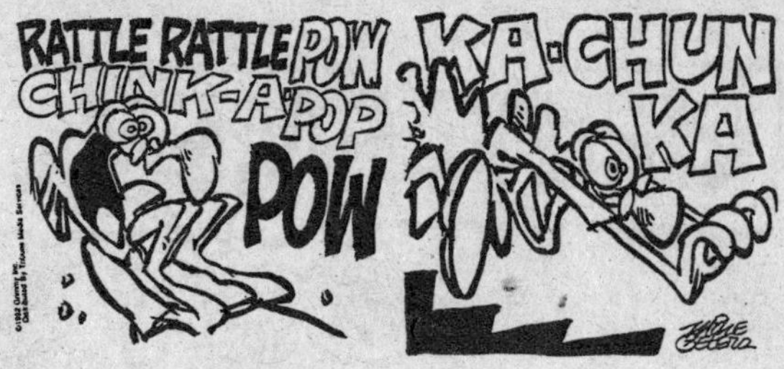
RATTLE RATTLE POW
CHINK-A-POP
POW
KA-CHUNKA

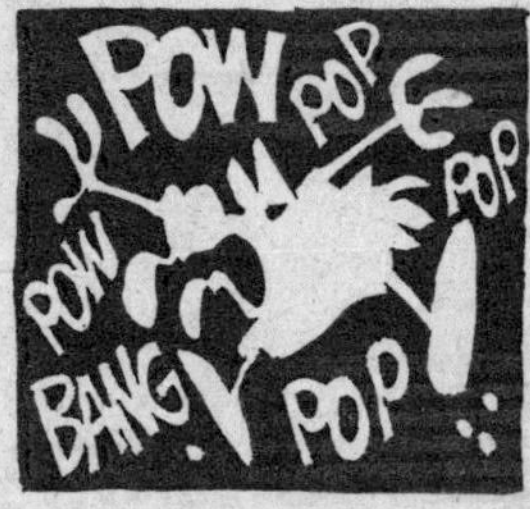
POW
POP
POP
POW
BANG
POP

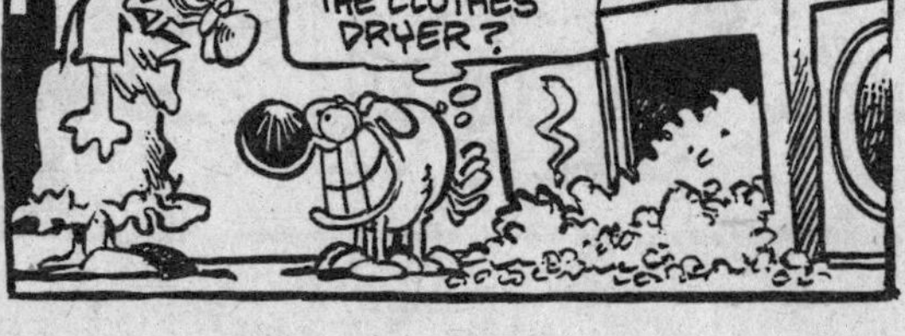
DID YOU KNOW YOU CAN POP CORN IN THE CLOTHES DRYER?

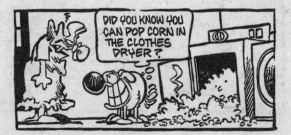

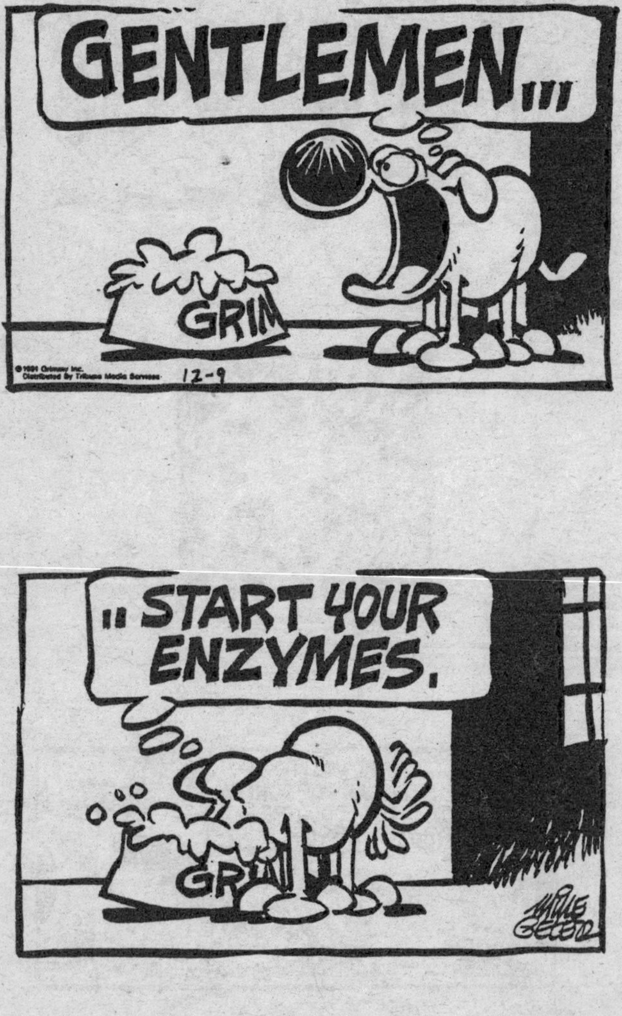
GENTLEMEN...
GRIM
© 1991 Grimmy Inc.
Distributed By Tribune Media Services
12-9
.. START YOUR ENZYMES.
GR

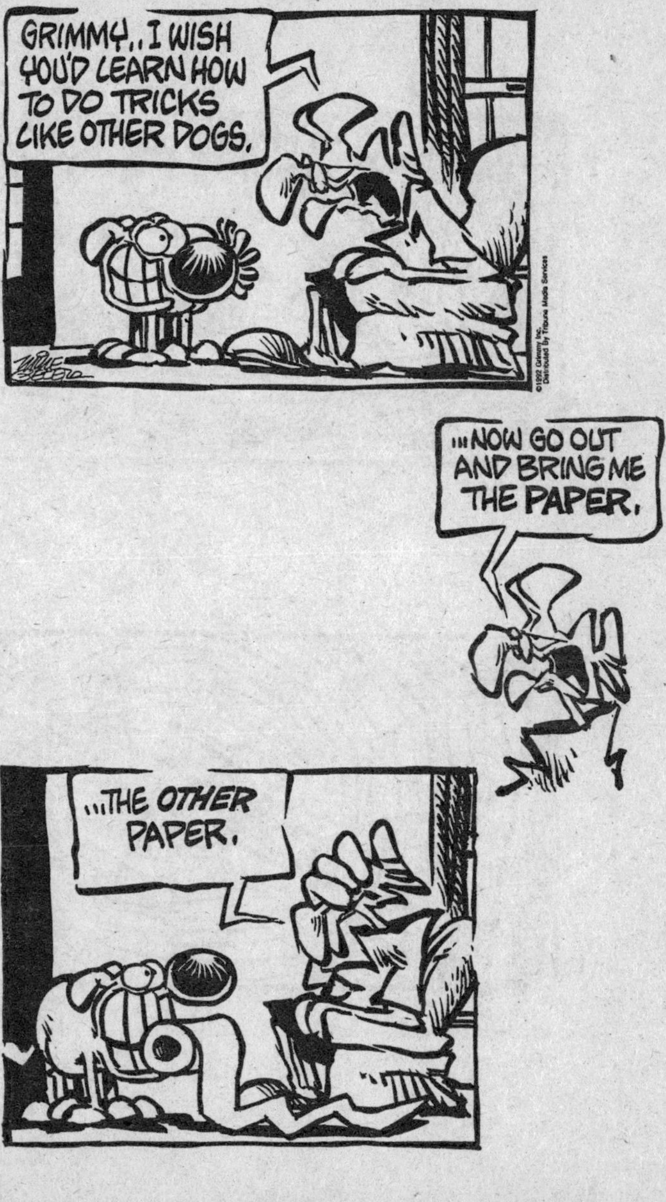
GRIMMY.. I WISH YOU'D LEARN HOW TO DO TRICKS LIKE OTHER DOGS.
©1992 Grimmy Inc. Distributed By Tribune Media Services
...NOW GO OUT AND BRING ME THE PAPER.
...THE OTHER PAPER.

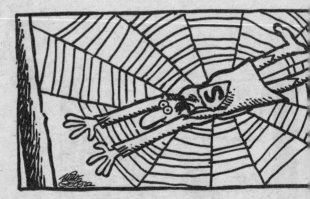

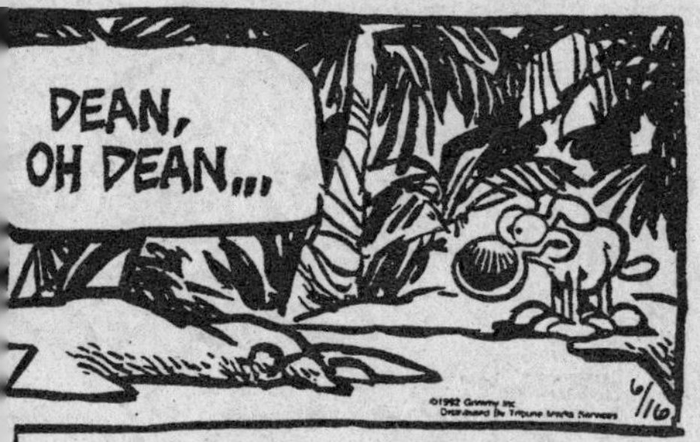
DEAN, OH DEAN...
6/16

MARTIN & LEWIS & CLARK EXPEDITION

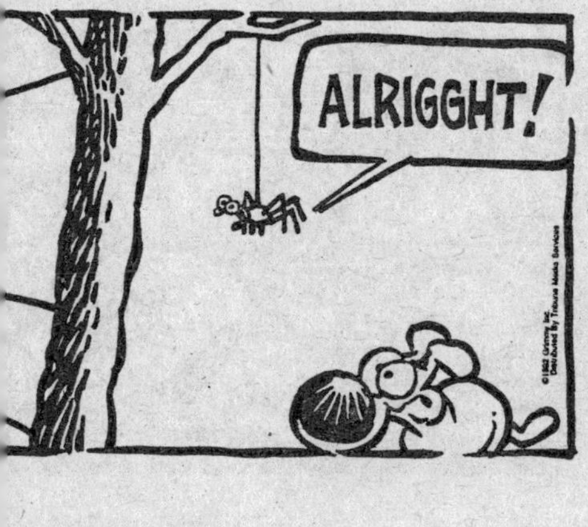
ALRIGGHT!

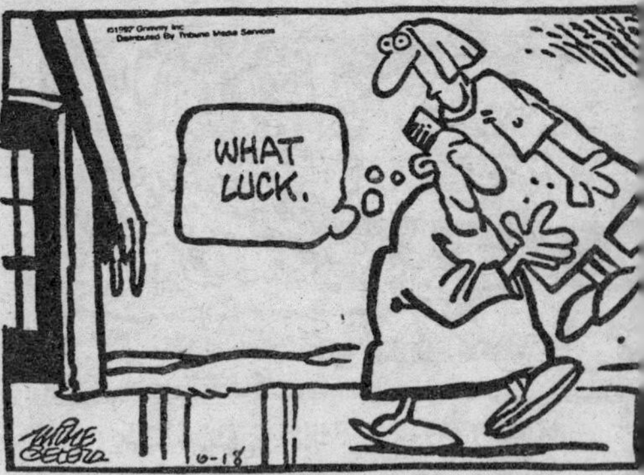
©1987 Grimmy Inc
Distributed By Tribune Media Services
WHAT LUCK.
6-18

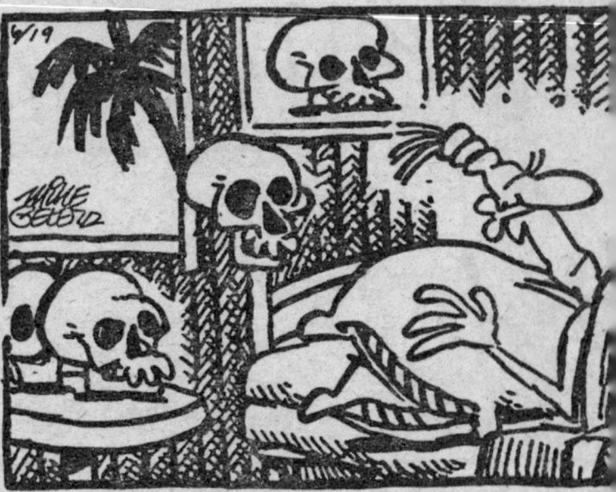
6/19

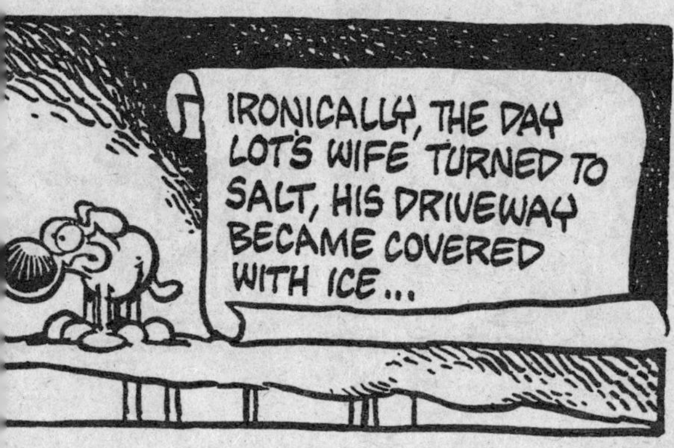
IRONICALLY, THE DAY LOT'S WIFE TURNED TO SALT, HIS DRIVEWAY BECAME COVERED WITH ICE...

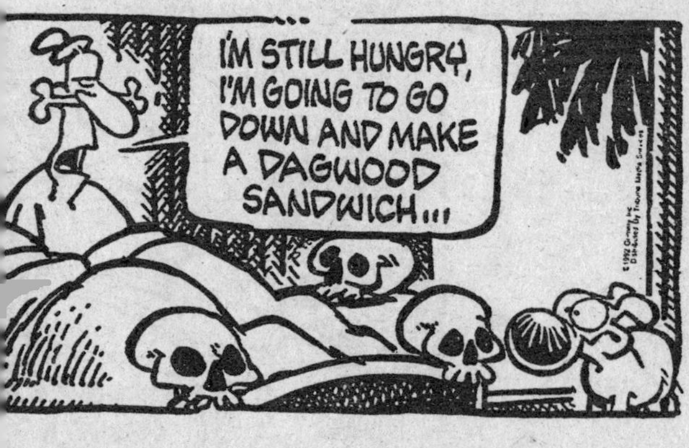
I'M STILL HUNGRY, I'M GOING TO GO DOWN AND MAKE A DAGWOOD SANDWICH...

PEG LEG
PETE

DEAD
EYE
DICK

BOY, GRIMMY,
GOOD THING I
SWERVED BACK
THERE, I ALMOST
HIT A SQUIRREL.

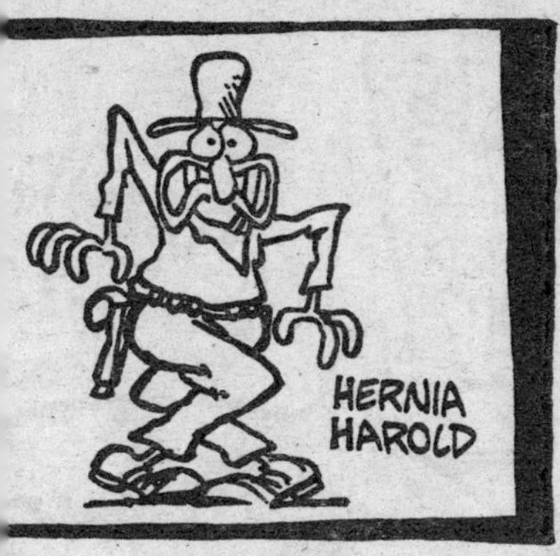
HERNIA
HAROLD

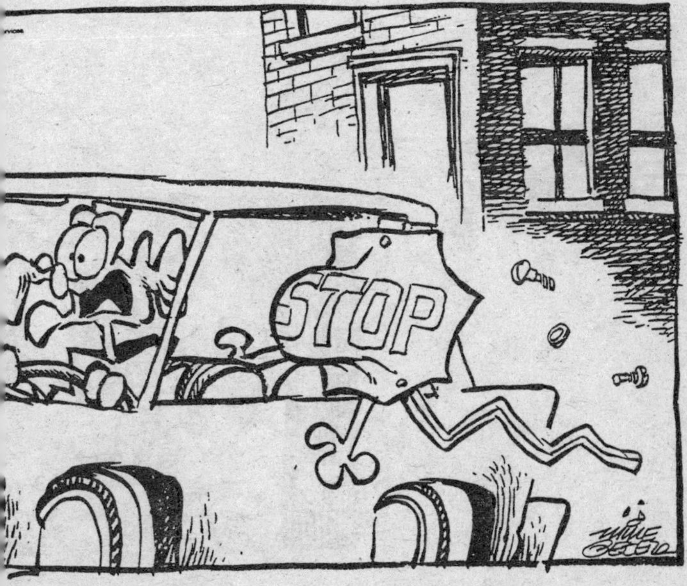
STOP

...AND MY FAVORITE IS THE CALIFORNIA ROLL, THAT'S A SURFER, COVERED IN COCONUT OIL, WRAPPED IN A RUBBER WET SUIT.

6-22

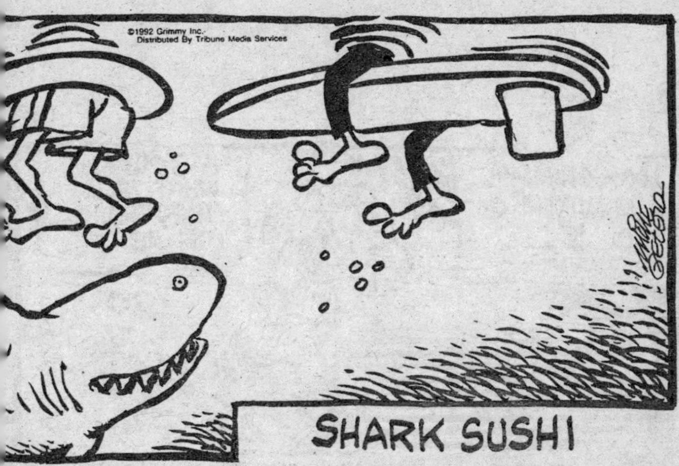
©1992 Grimmy Inc.
Distributed By Tribune Media Services

SHARK SUSHI

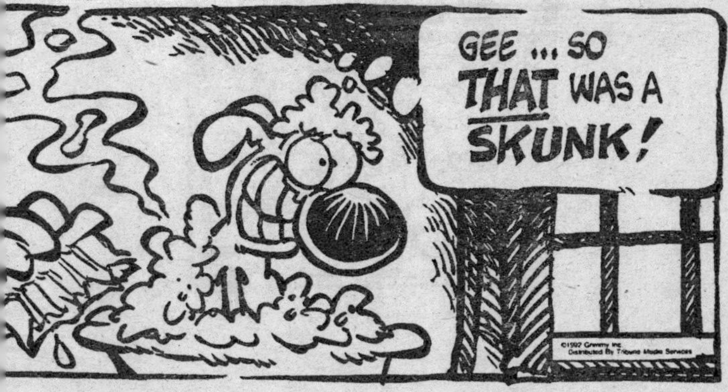
GEE ... SO **THAT** WAS A **SKUNK**!
©1992 Grimmy Inc.
Distributed By Tribune Media Services

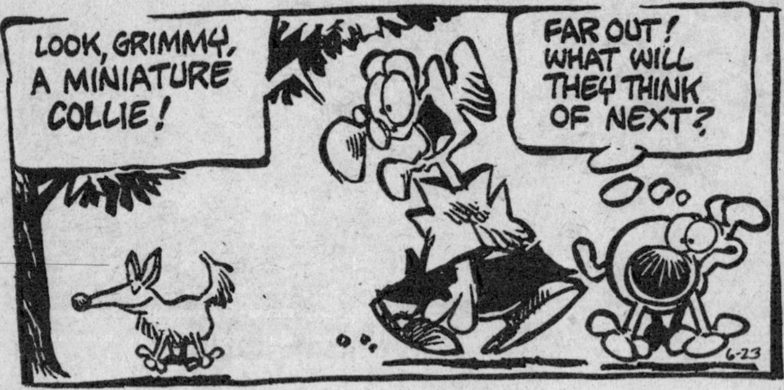
LOOK, GRIMMY, A MINIATURE COLLIE!
FAR OUT! WHAT WILL THEY THINK OF NEXT?
6-23

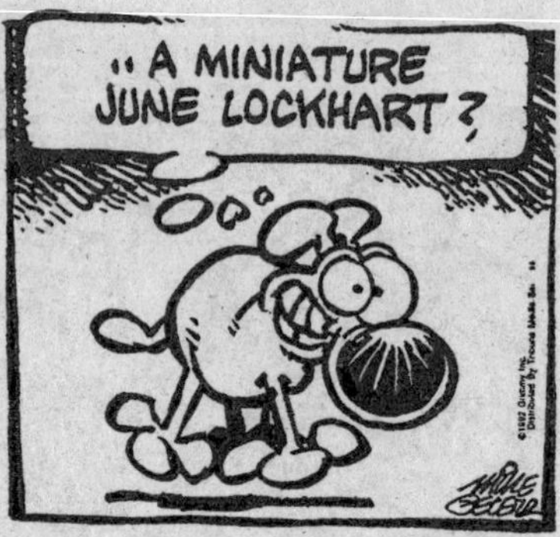
.. A MINIATURE JUNE LOCKHART?

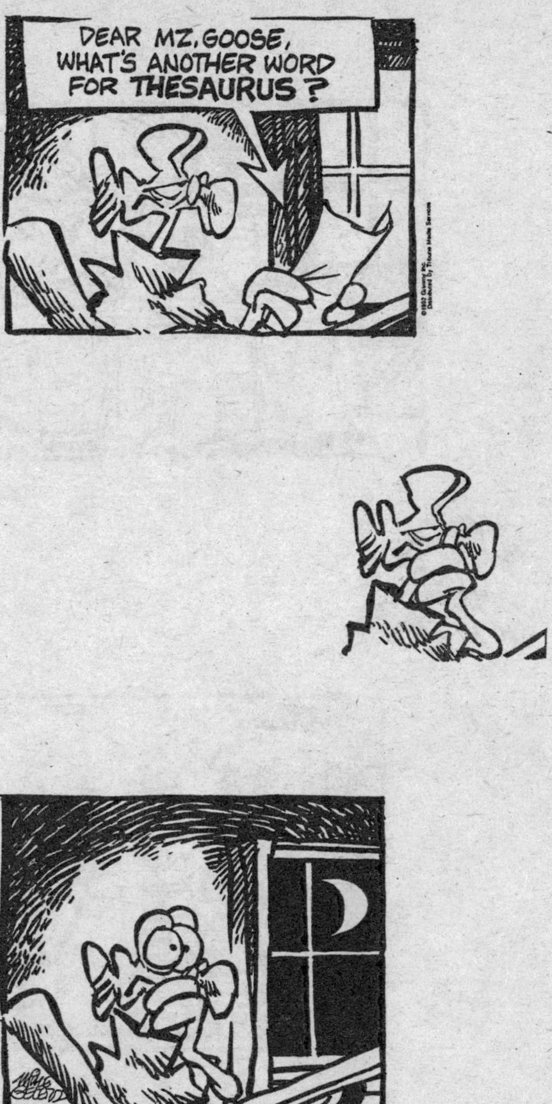
DEAR MZ. GOOSE,
WHAT'S ANOTHER WORD
FOR THESAURUS?

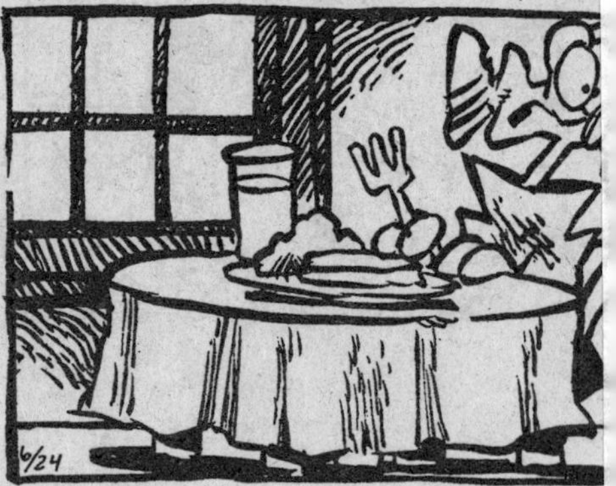
6/24

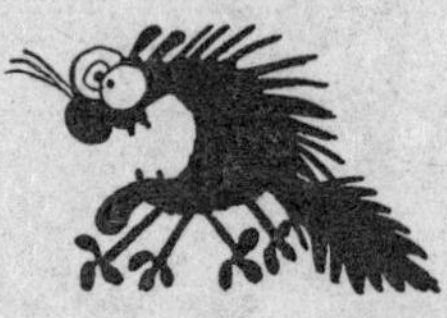

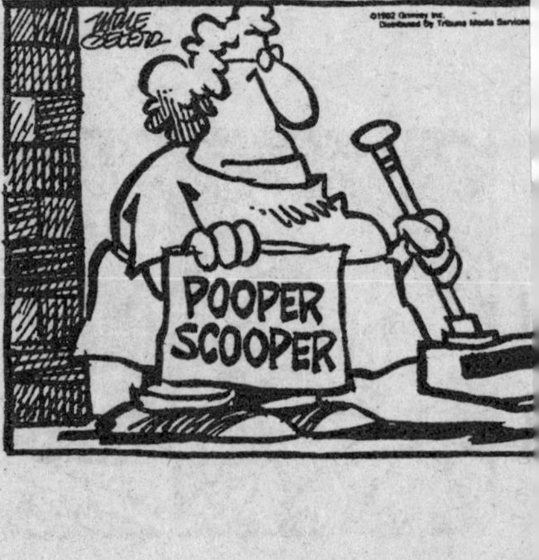
©1992 Grimmy Inc.
Distributed by Tribune Media Services
POOPER
SCOOPER

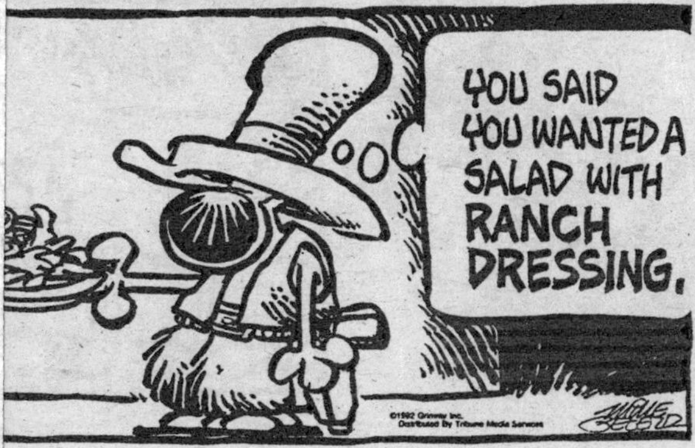
YOU SAID YOU WANTED A SALAD WITH RANCH DRESSING.
©1992 Grimmy Inc.
Distributed By Tribune Media Services

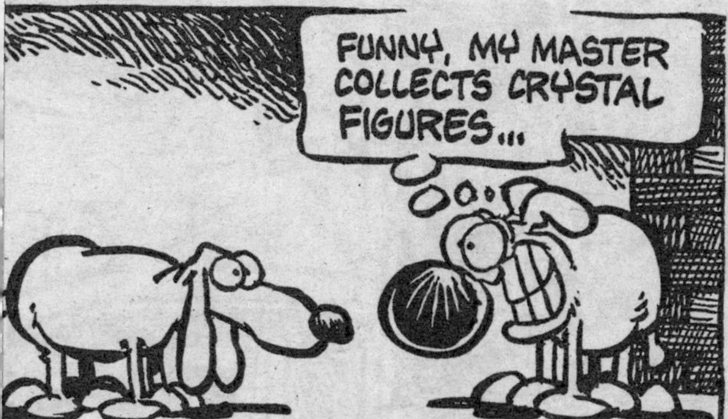
FUNNY, MY MASTER COLLECTS CRYSTAL FIGURES...

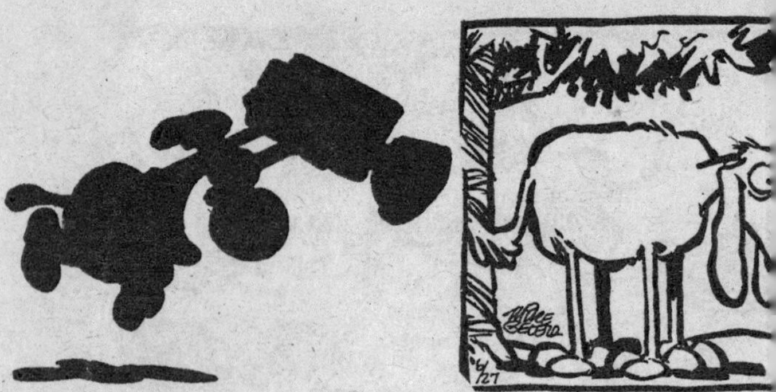

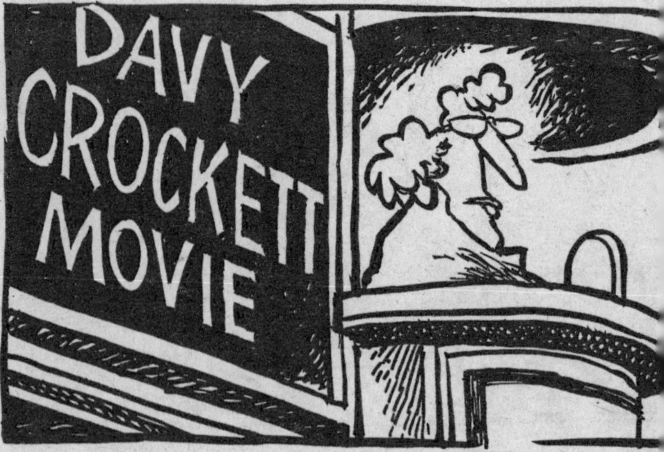
DAVY CROCKETT MOVIE

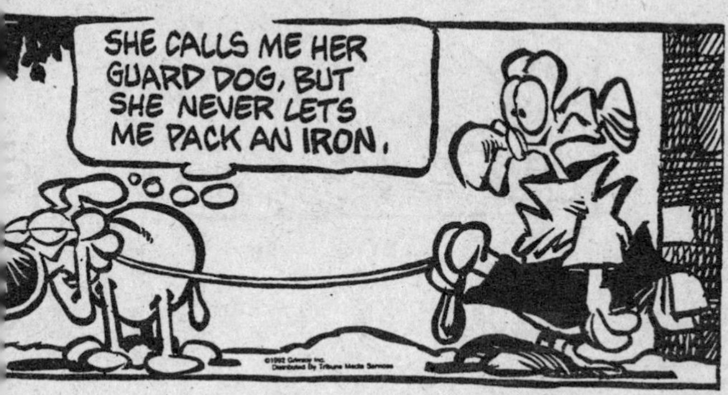
SHE CALLS ME HER GUARD DOG, BUT SHE NEVER LETS ME PACK AN IRON.
©1992 Grimmy Inc. Distributed By Tribune Media Services

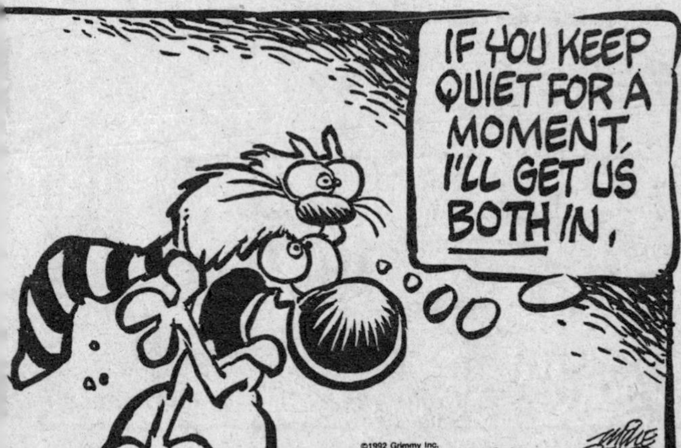
IF YOU KEEP QUIET FOR A MOMENT, I'LL GET US BOTH IN.
©1992 Grimmy Inc. Distributed By Tribune Media Services
MIKE PETERS

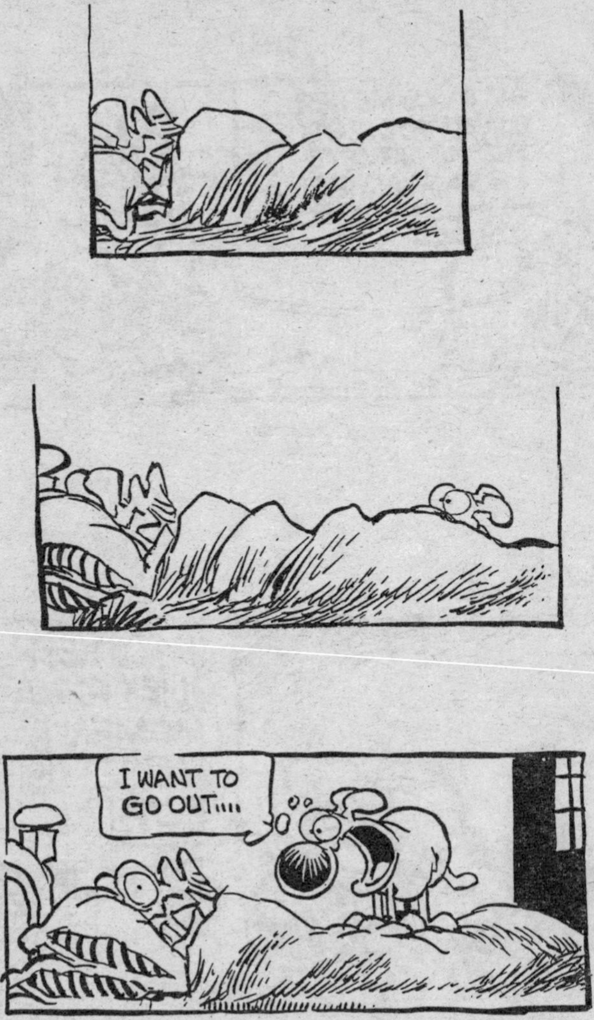
I WANT TO GO OUT....

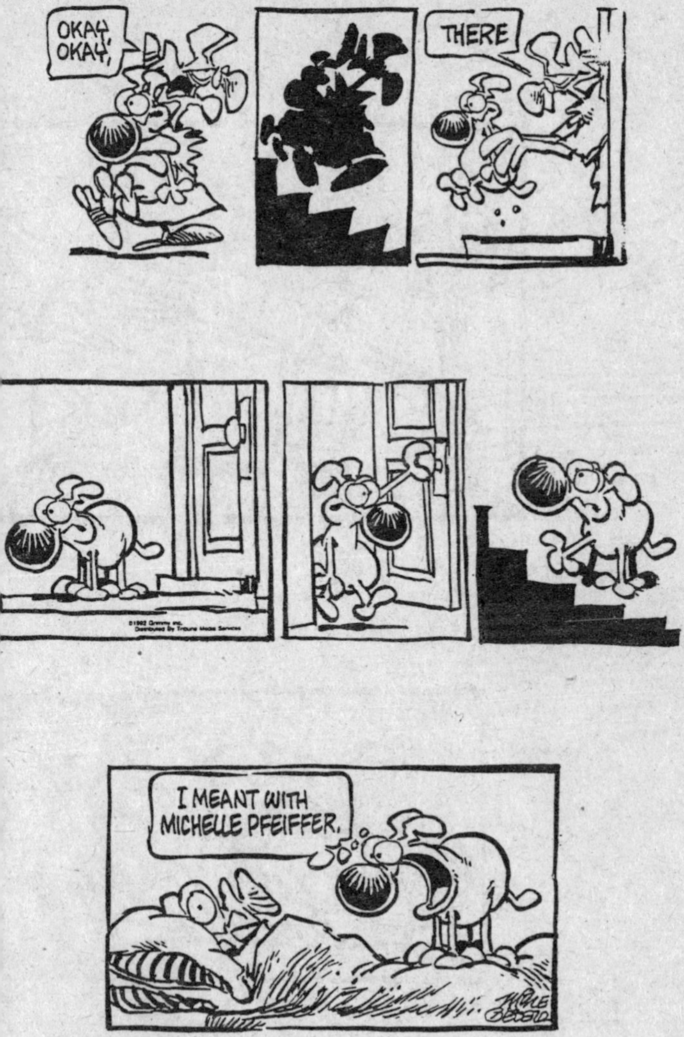
OKAY, OKAY,
THERE
I MEANT WITH MICHELLE PFEIFFER.

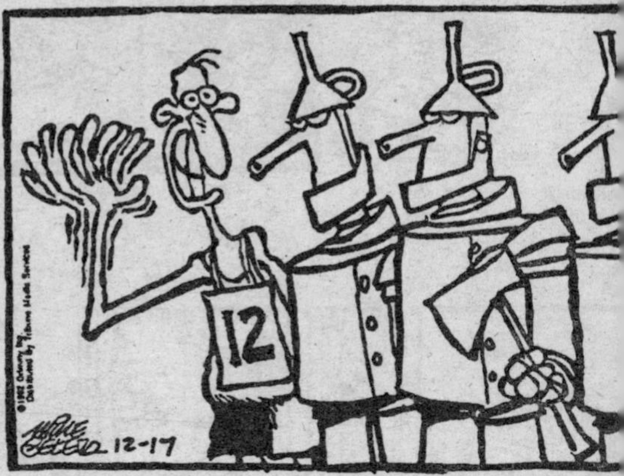
©1992 Grimmy Inc.
Distributed by Tribune Media Services
12
12-17

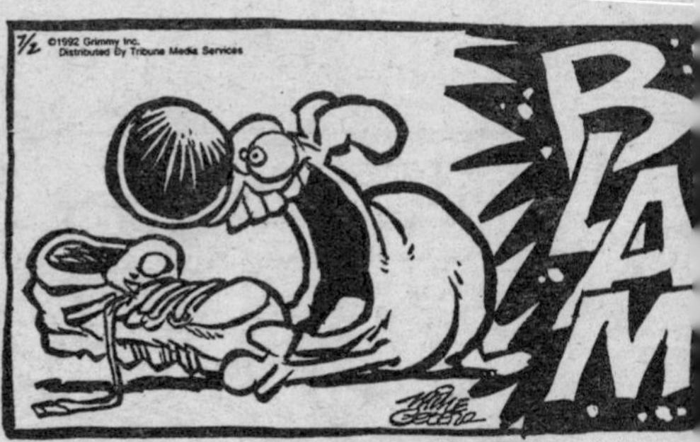
7/2
©1992 Grimmy Inc.
Distributed by Tribune Media Services

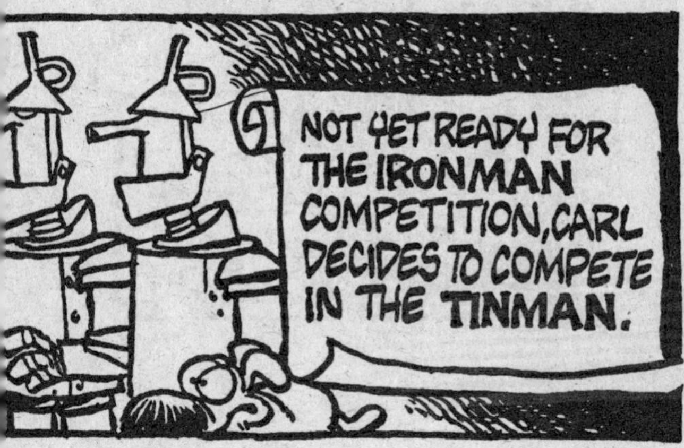
NOT YET READY FOR THE IRONMAN COMPETITION, CARL DECIDES TO COMPETE IN THE TINMAN.

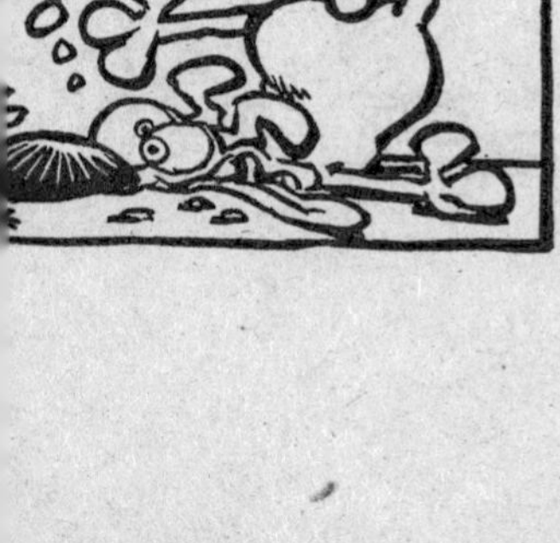
NEVER CHEW A FULLY INFLATED REEBOK.

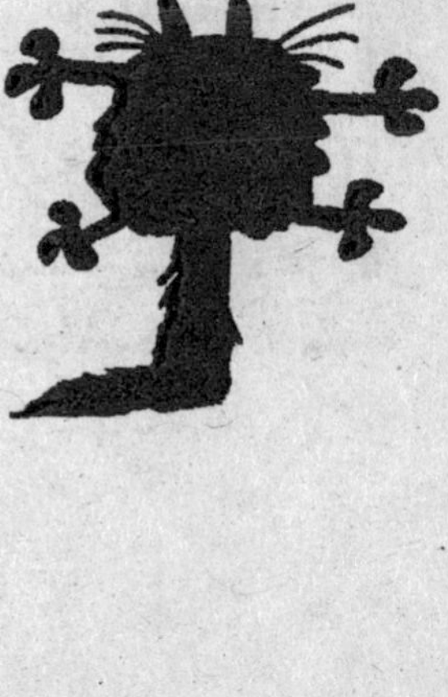

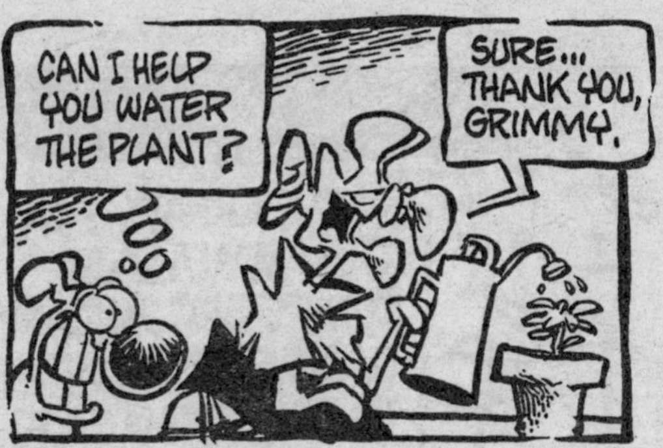
CAN I HELP YOU WATER THE PLANT?
SURE... THANK YOU, GRIMMY.

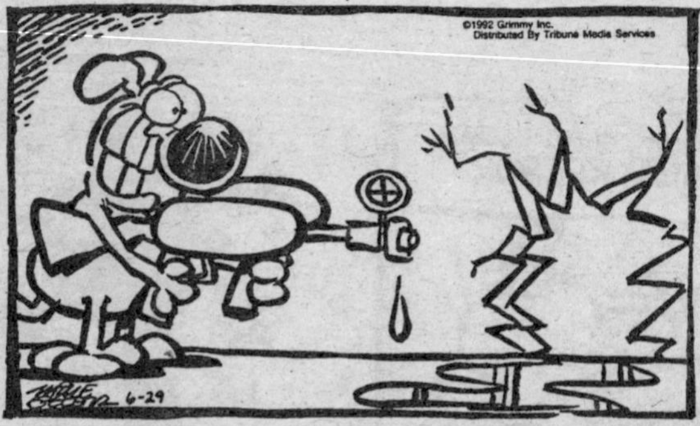
©1992 Grimmy Inc.
Distributed By Tribune Media Services
6-29

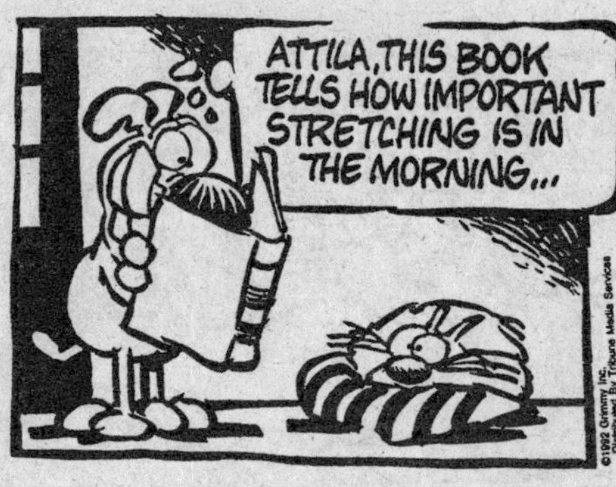
ATTILA, THIS BOOK TELLS HOW IMPORTANT STRETCHING IS IN THE MORNING...
©1992 Grimmy Inc.
Distributed By Tribune Media Services

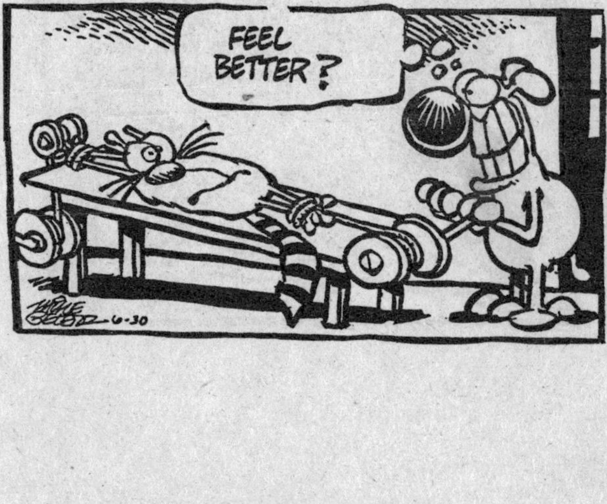
FEEL BETTER?

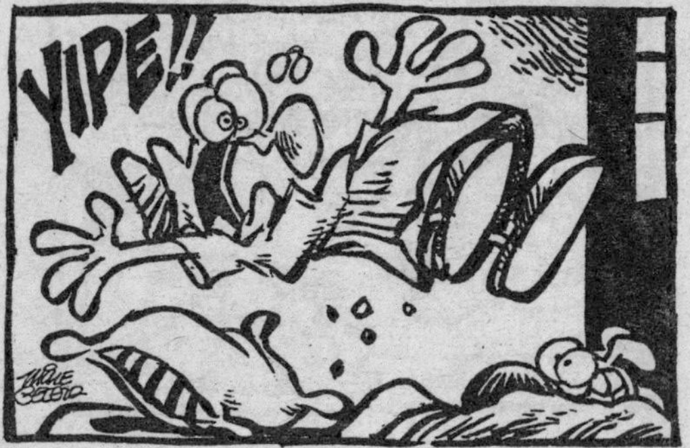
YIPE!!

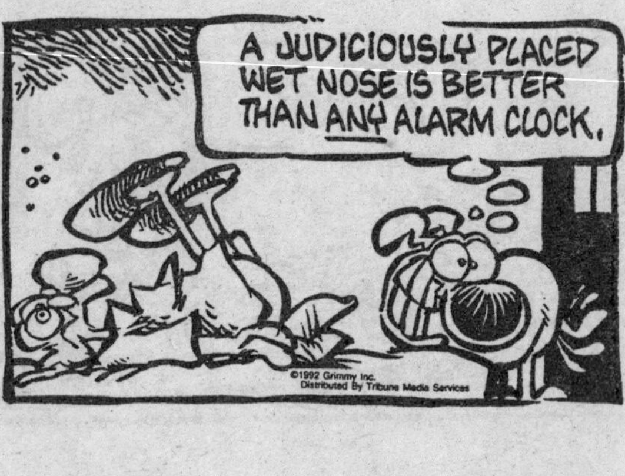
A JUDICIOUSLY PLACED WET NOSE IS BETTER THAN ANY ALARM CLOCK.
©1992 Grimmy Inc.
Distributed By Tribune Media Services

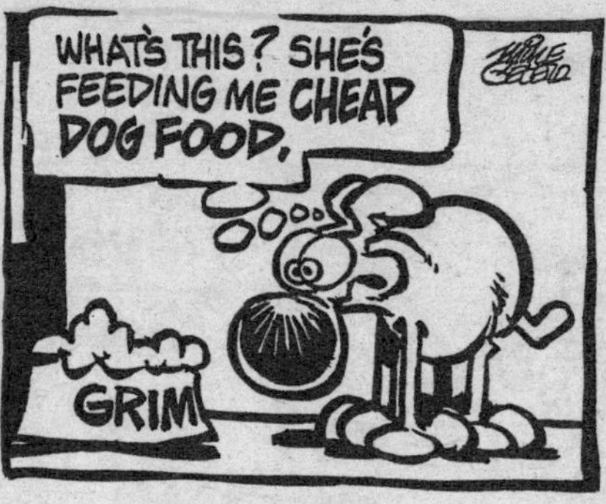
WHAT'S THIS? SHE'S FEEDING ME CHEAP DOG FOOD.
GRIM

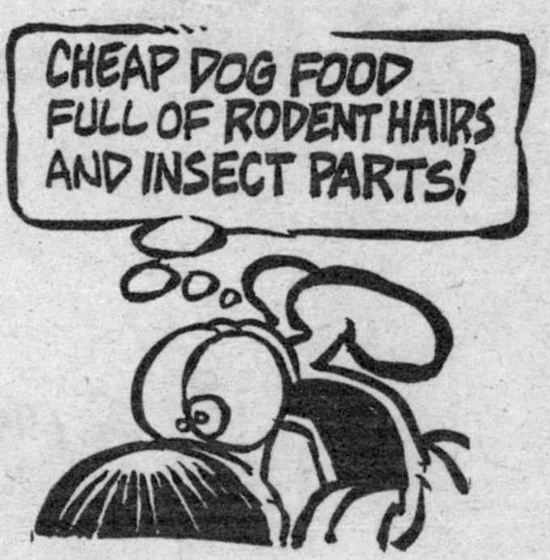
CHEAP DOG FOOD FULL OF RODENT HAIRS AND INSECT PARTS!

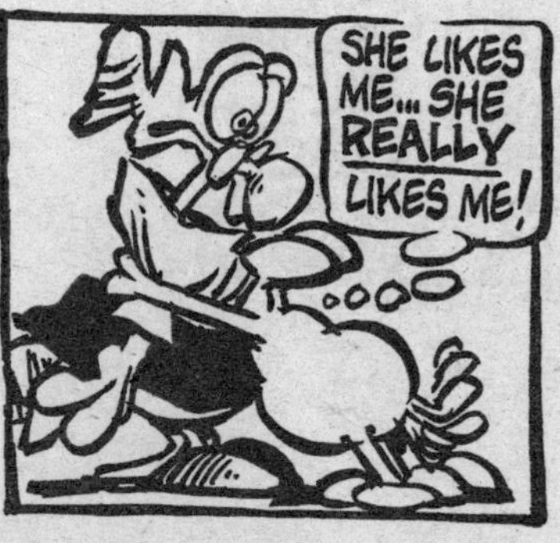
SHE LIKES ME... SHE REALLY LIKES ME!

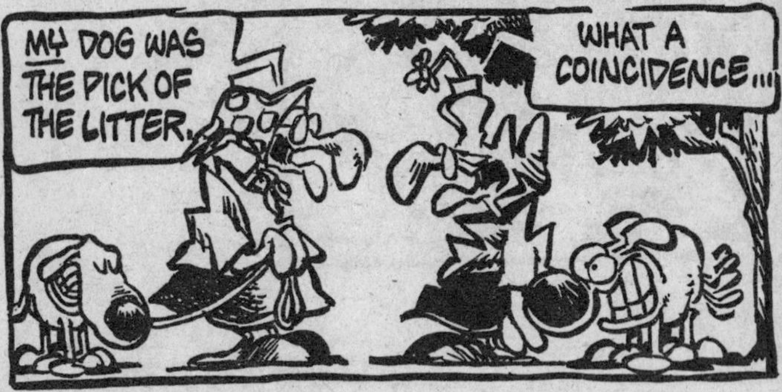
MY DOG WAS THE PICK OF THE LITTER.
WHAT A COINCIDENCE...

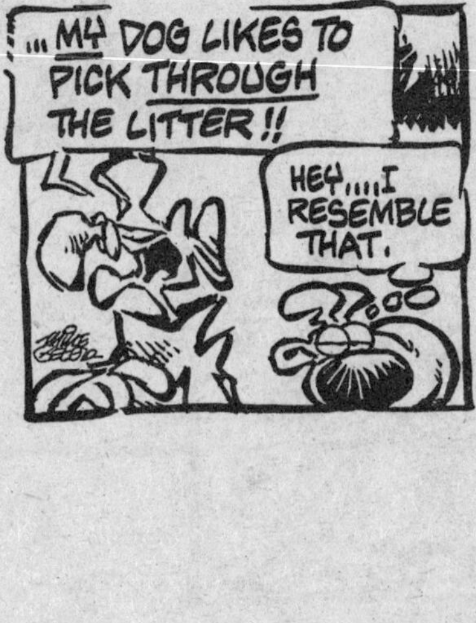
...MY DOG LIKES TO PICK THROUGH THE LITTER!!
HEY....I RESEMBLE THAT.

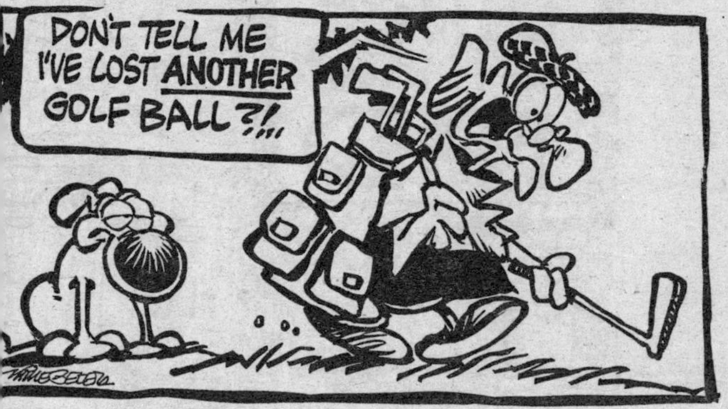
DON'T TELL ME I'VE LOST ANOTHER GOLF BALL?!

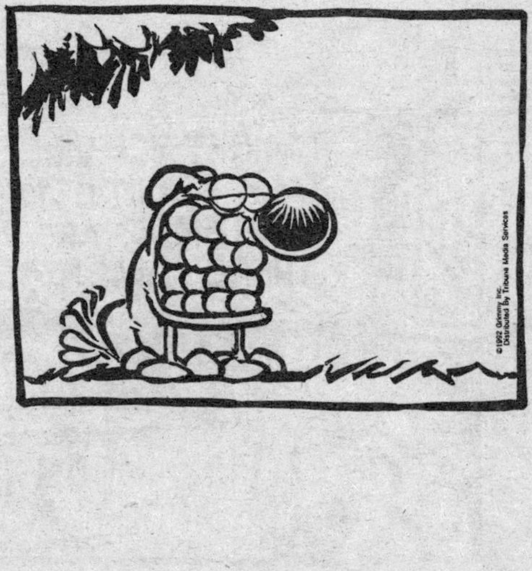
©1992 Grimmy Inc.
Distributed by Tribune Media Services

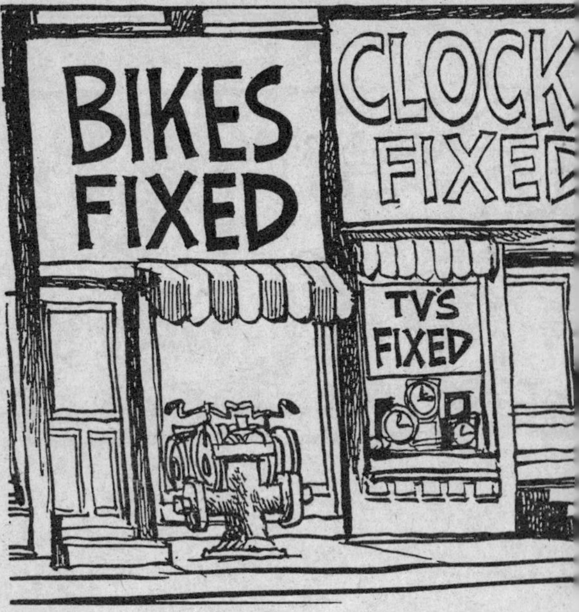
BIKES FIXED
CLOCK FIXED
TV'S FIXED

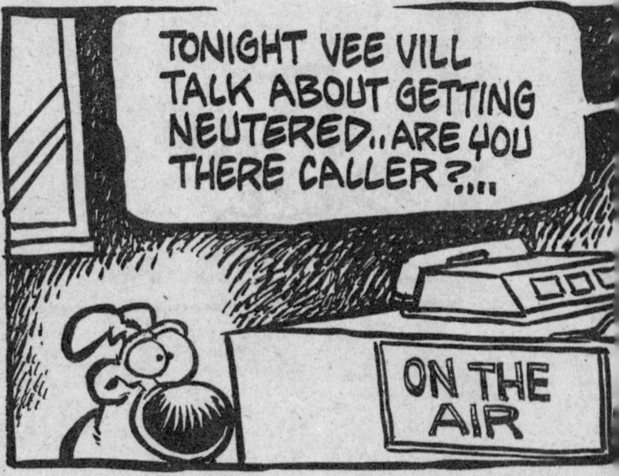
TONIGHT VEE VILL TALK ABOUT GETTING NEUTERED.. ARE YOU THERE CALLER?...
ON THE AIR

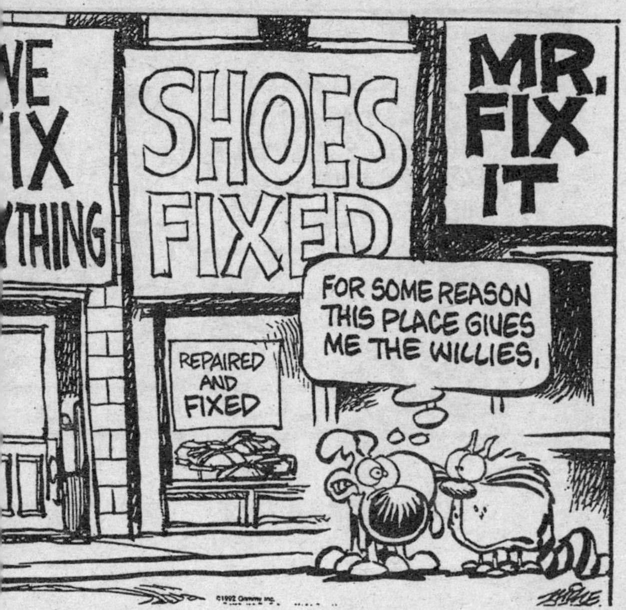
VE
IX
YTHING
SHOES FIXED
MR. FIX IT
REPAIRED AND FIXED
FOR SOME REASON THIS PLACE GIVES ME THE WILLIES.
©1992 Grimmy Inc.

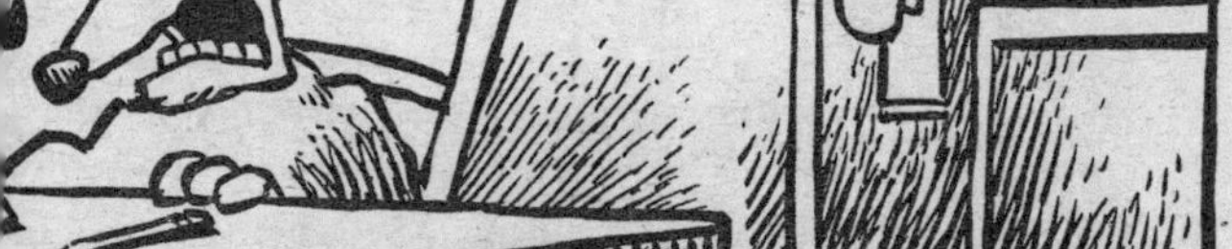
©1992 Grimmy Inc.
Distributed By Tribune Media Services
DR. RUTH ROTTWEILER

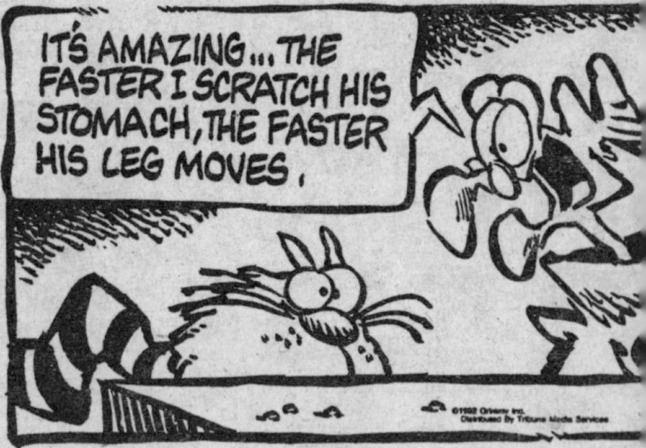
IT'S AMAZING... THE FASTER I SCRATCH HIS STOMACH, THE FASTER HIS LEG MOVES.
©1992 Grimmy Inc.
Distributed By Tribune Media Services

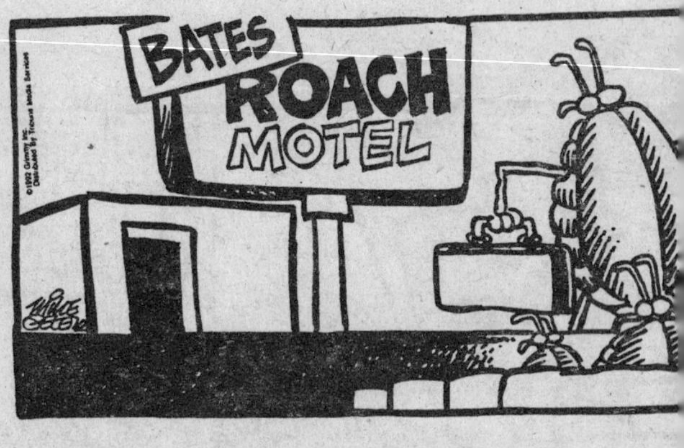
BATES
ROACH
MOTEL
©1992 Grimmy Inc.
Distributed By Tribune Media Services

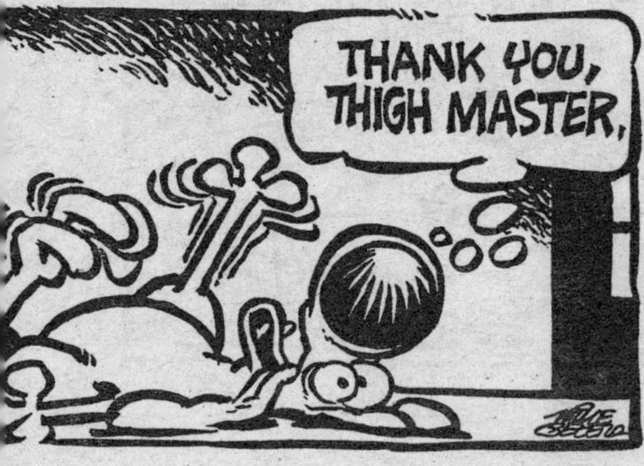
THANK YOU, THIGH MASTER.

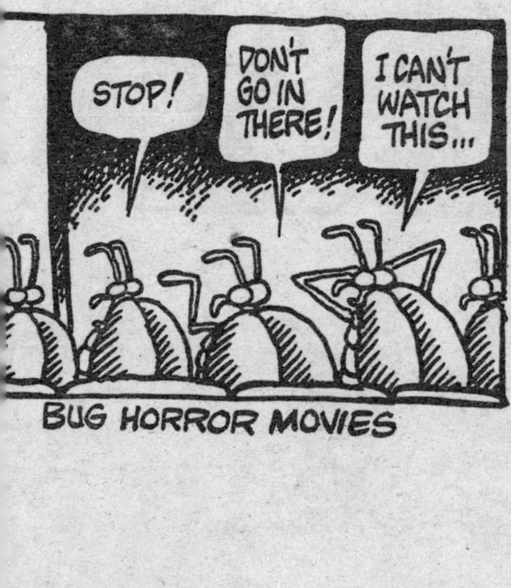
STOP!
DON'T GO IN THERE!
I CAN'T WATCH THIS...

BUG HORROR MOVIES

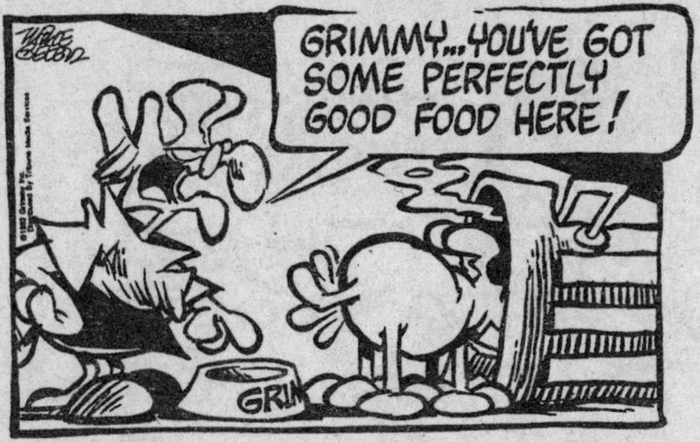
GRIMMY...YOU'VE GOT SOME PERFECTLY GOOD FOOD HERE!
GRIM

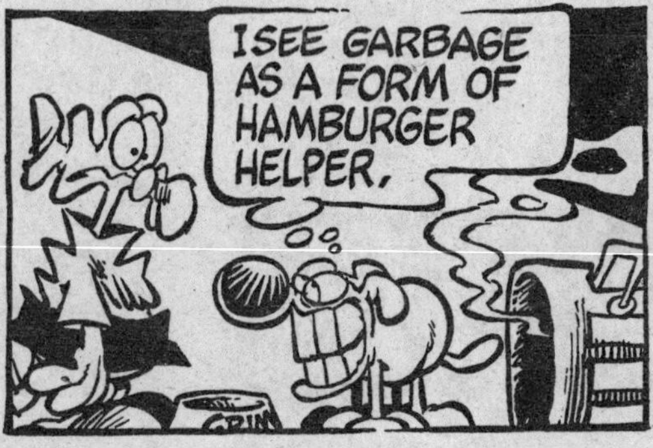
I SEE GARBAGE AS A FORM OF HAMBURGER HELPER.
GRIM

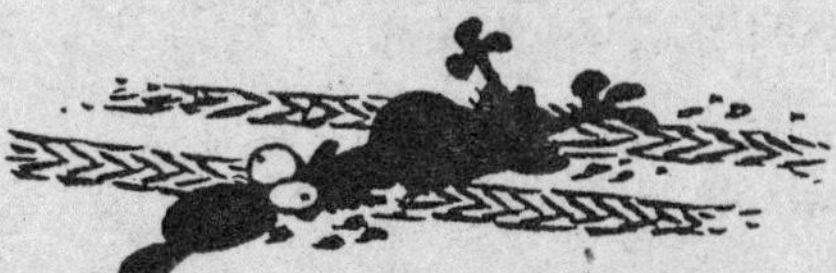

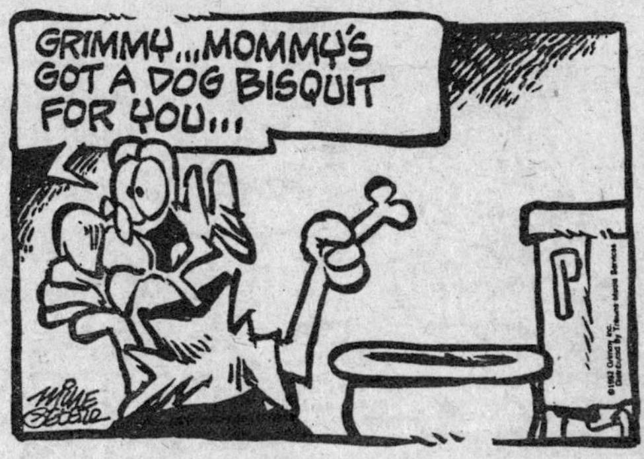
GRIMMY...MOMMY'S GOT A DOG BISQUIT FOR YOU...

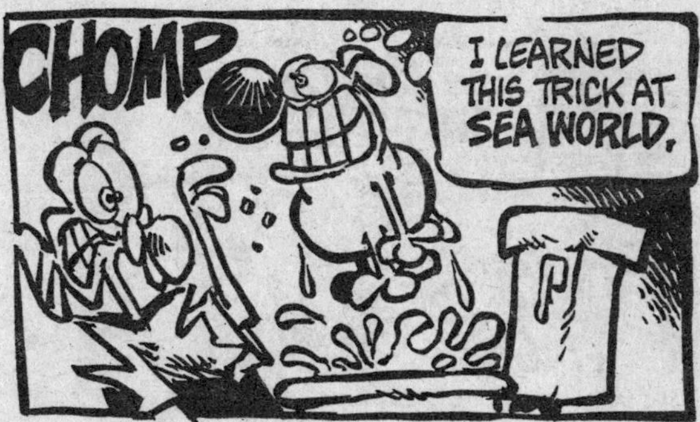
CHOMP
I LEARNED THIS TRICK AT SEA WORLD.

LOOK, GRIMMY... HERE'S SOME NICE, YUMMY DOG FOOD...
...MY COMPLIMENTS TO THE CAN.

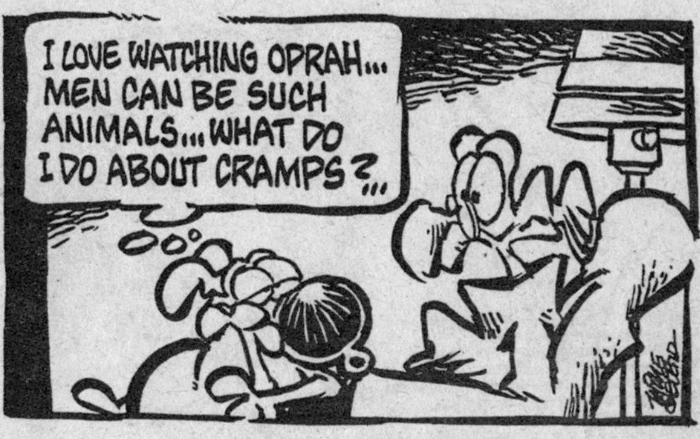
I LOVE WATCHING OPRAH... MEN CAN BE SUCH ANIMALS... WHAT DO I DO ABOUT CRAMPS?...

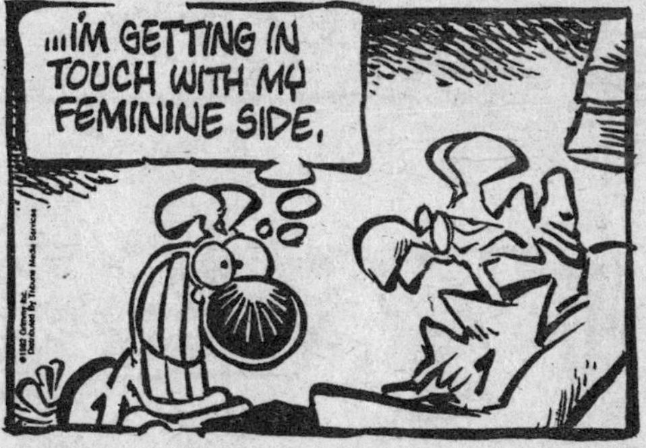
...I'M GETTING IN TOUCH WITH MY FEMININE SIDE.

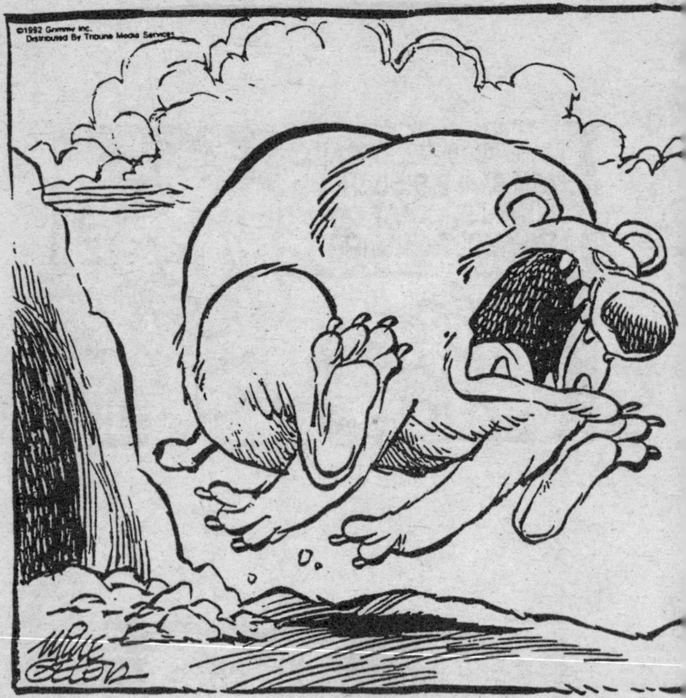
©1992 Grimmy Inc.
Distributed By Tribune Media Services

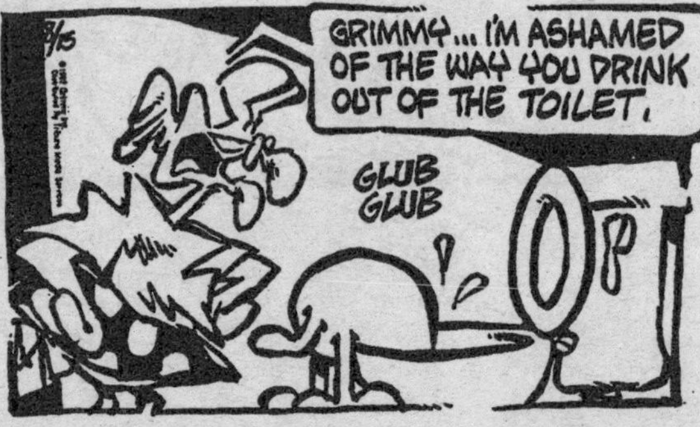
GRIMMY... I'M ASHAMED OF THE WAY YOU DRINK OUT OF THE TOILET.
GLUB GLUB

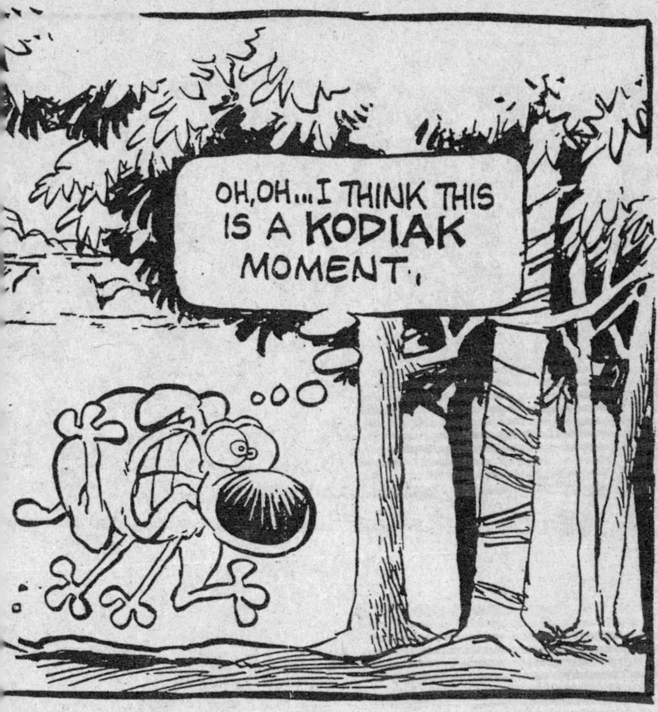
OH, OH... I THINK THIS IS A KODIAK MOMENT.

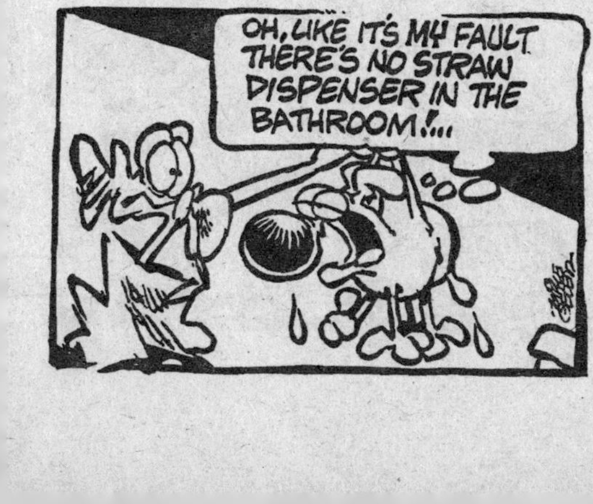
OH, LIKE IT'S MY FAULT THERE'S NO STRAW DISPENSER IN THE BATHROOM!...

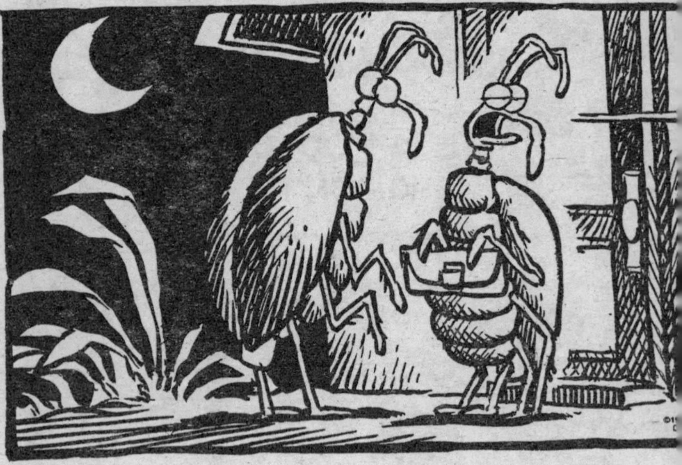

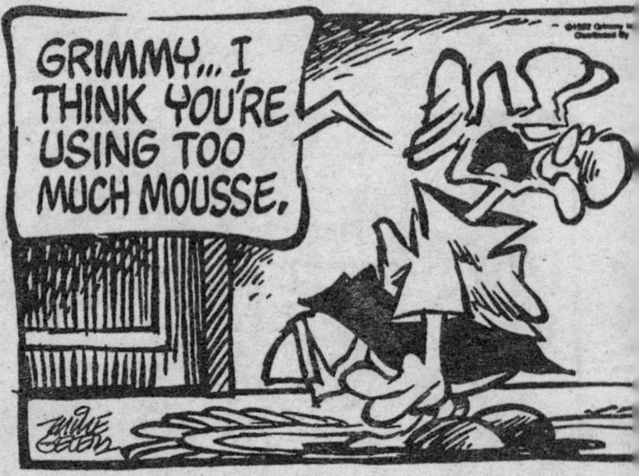
GRIMMY... I THINK YOU'RE USING TOO MUCH MOUSSE.

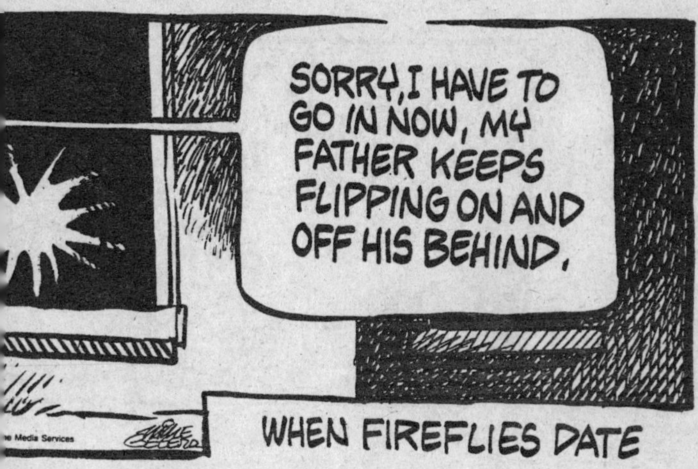
SORRY, I HAVE TO GO IN NOW, MY FATHER KEEPS FLIPPING ON AND OFF HIS BEHIND.
e Media Services

WHEN FIREFLIES DATE

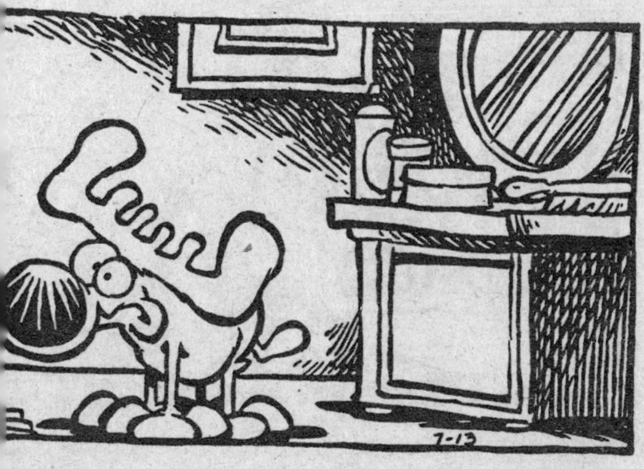
7-13

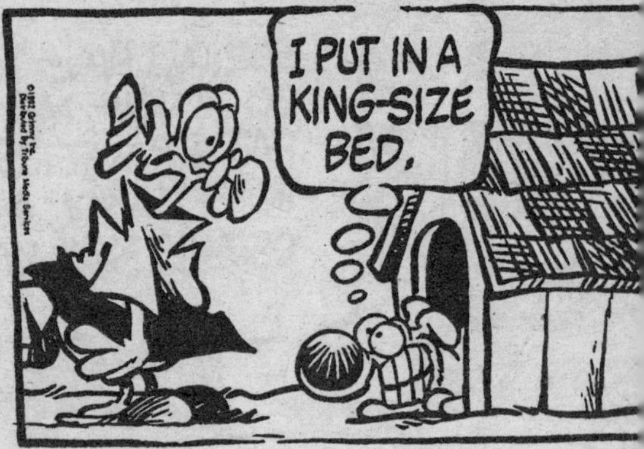
©1982 Grimmy Inc.
Distributed by Tribune Media Services
I PUT IN A KING-SIZE BED.

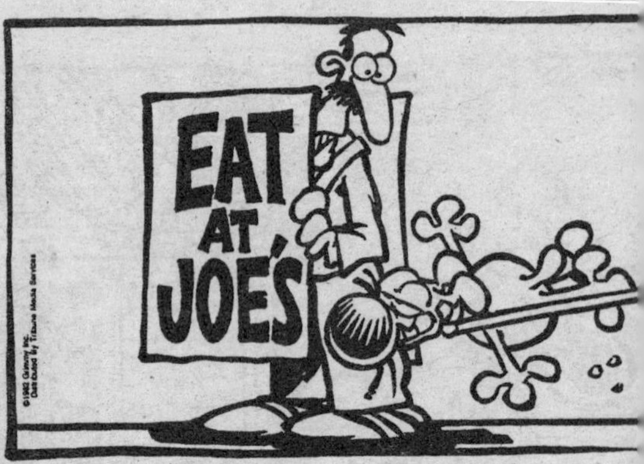
©1982 Grimmy Inc.
Distributed by Tribune Media Services
EAT AT JOE'S

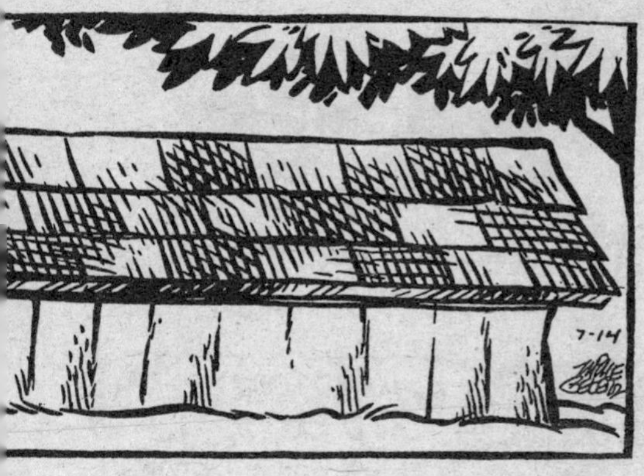
7-14

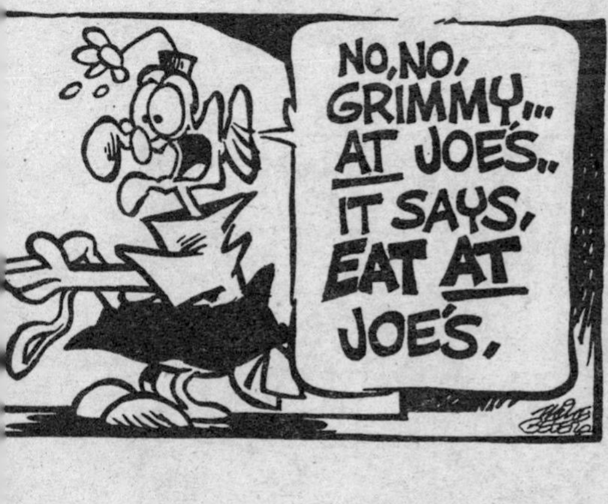
NO, NO, GRIMMY... AT JOE'S.. IT SAYS, EAT AT JOE'S.

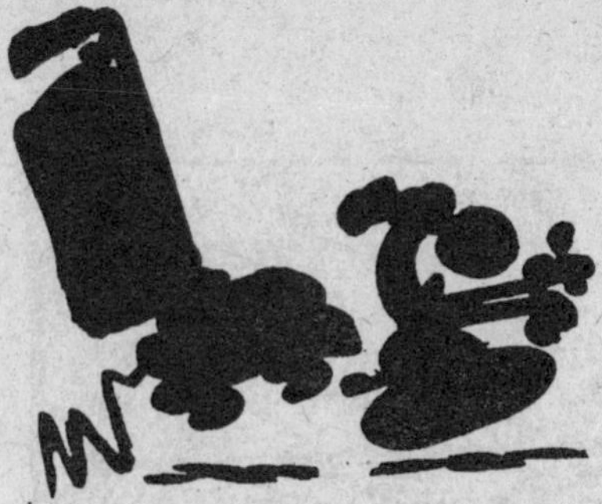

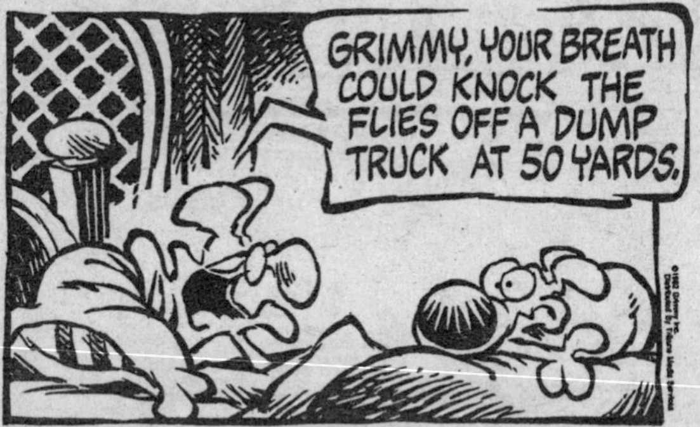
GRIMMY, YOUR BREATH COULD KNOCK THE FLIES OFF A DUMP TRUCK AT 50 YARDS.

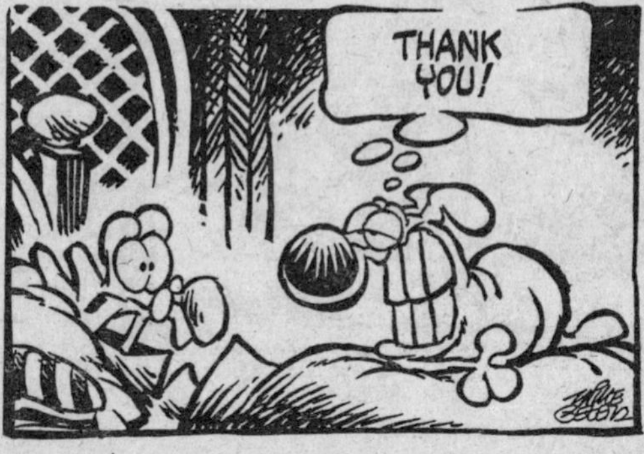
THANK YOU!

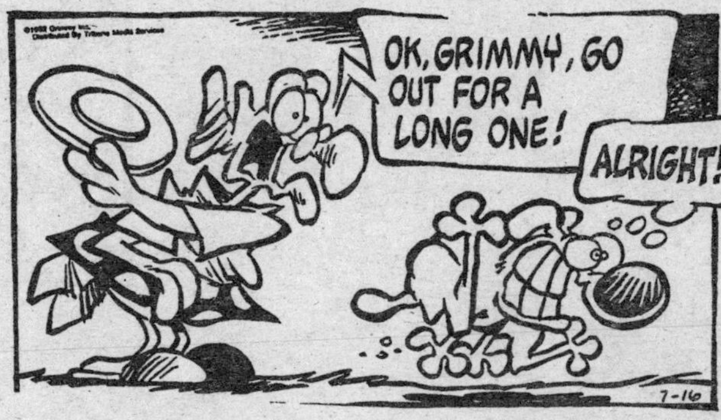
OK, GRIMMY, GO OUT FOR A LONG ONE!
ALRIGHT!
7-16

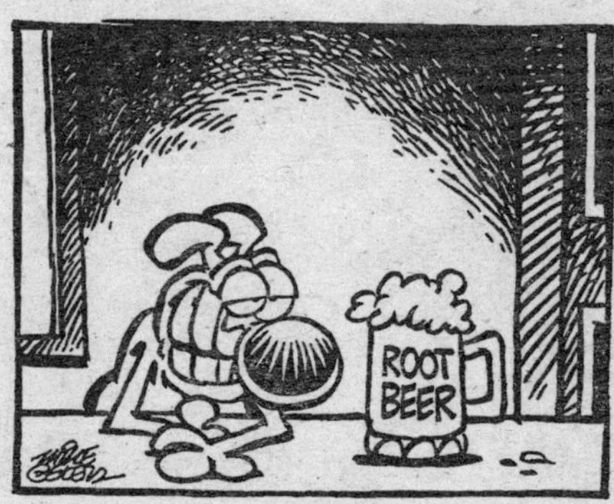
ROOT BEER

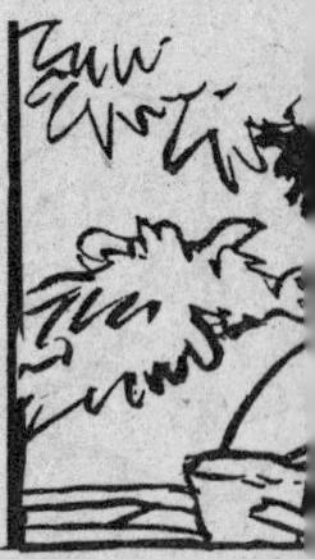

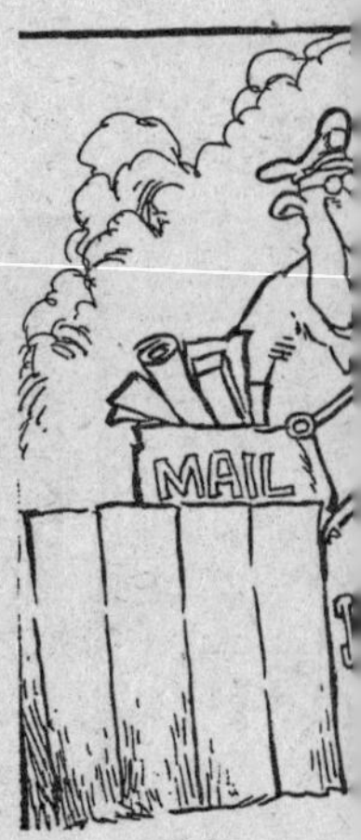
MAIL

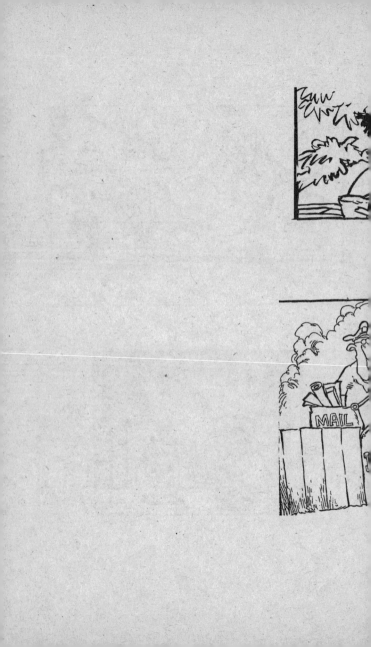

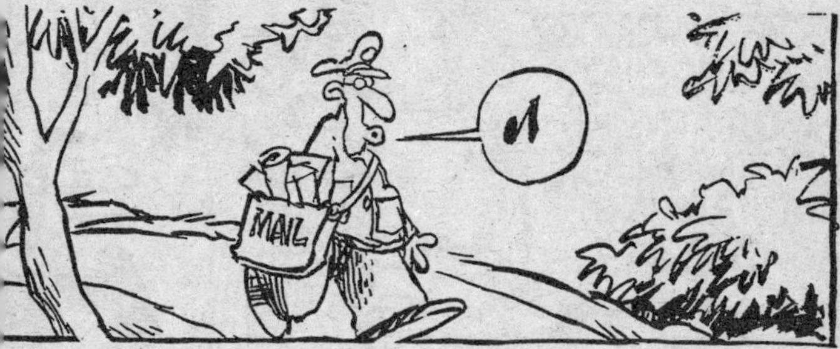
MAIL

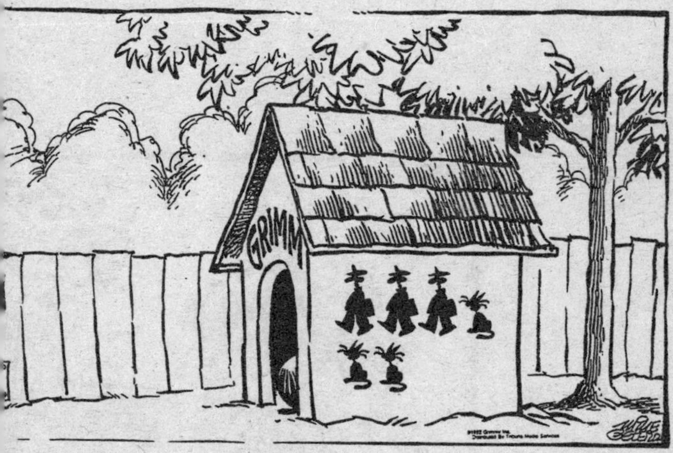
GRIMM

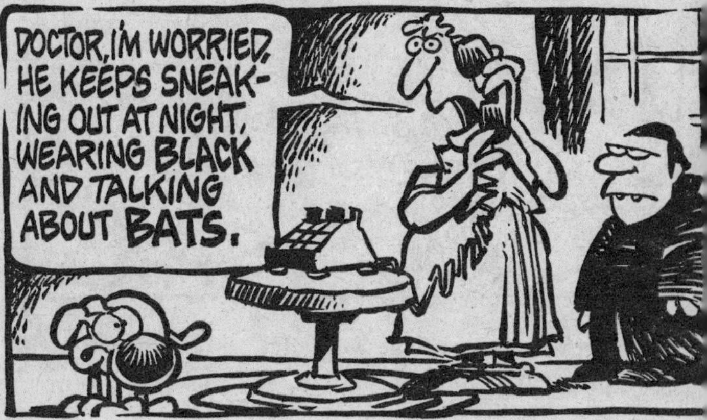
DOCTOR, I'M WORRIED, HE KEEPS SNEAKING OUT AT NIGHT, WEARING BLACK AND TALKING ABOUT BATS.

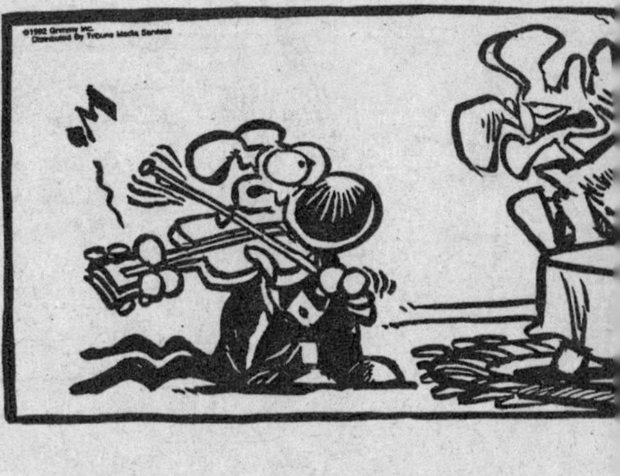
©1992 Grimmy Inc.
Distributed by Tribune Media Services

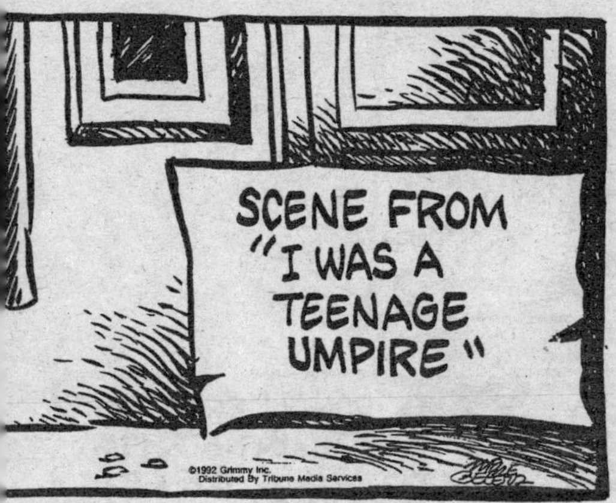

SCENE FROM "I WAS A TEENAGE UMPIRE"
©1992 Grimmy Inc.
Distributed By Tribune Media Services

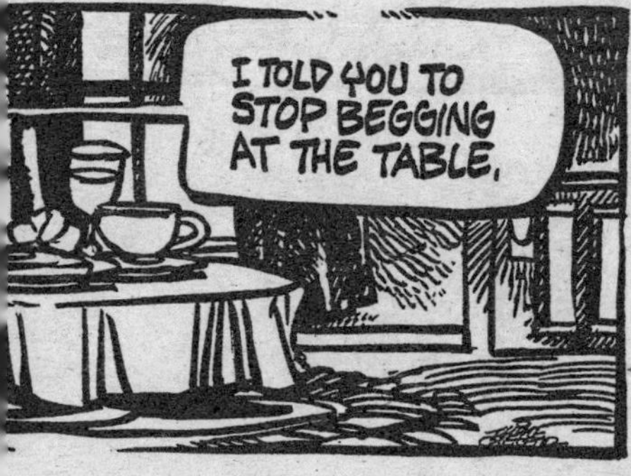

I TOLD YOU TO STOP BEGGING AT THE TABLE.

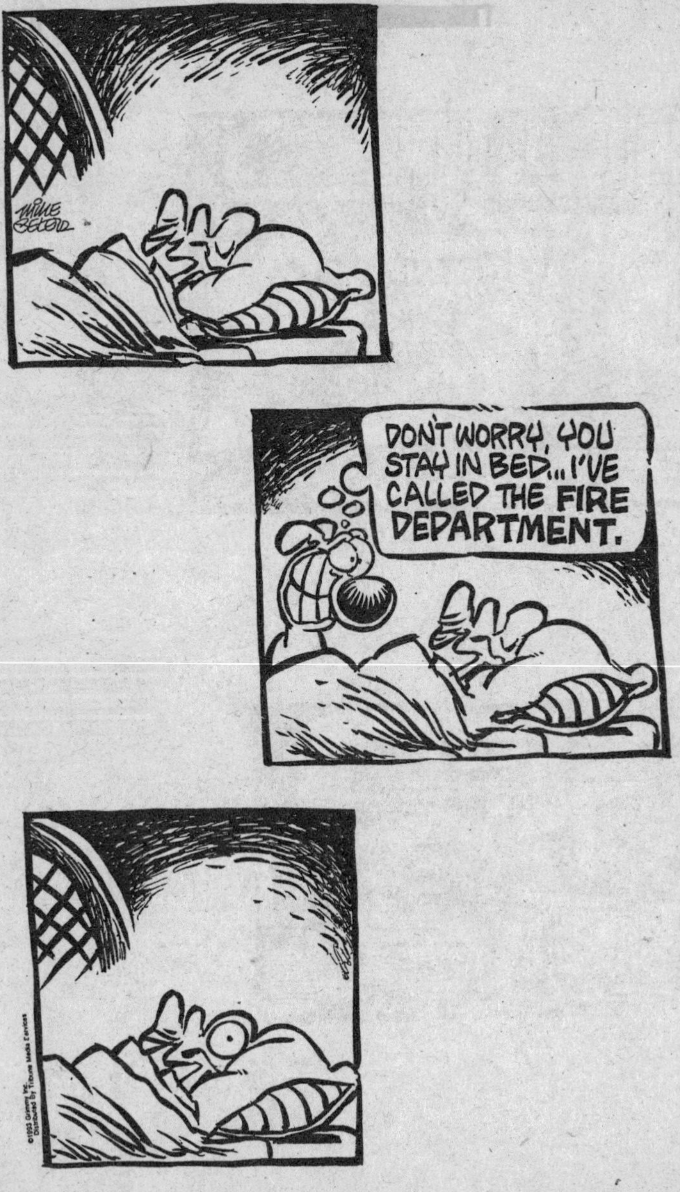
DON'T WORRY, YOU STAY IN BED... I'VE CALLED THE FIRE DEPARTMENT.
©1993 Grimmy Inc. Distributed By Tribune Media Services

OKAY, GRIMMY, JUMP UP, JUMP UP,...
PAT PAT PAT
7/30
.. NOT THAT FAR UP.

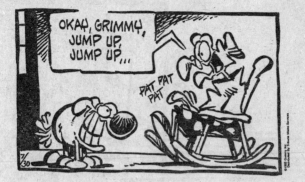

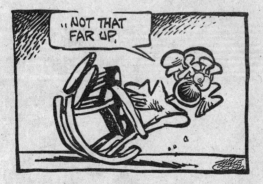

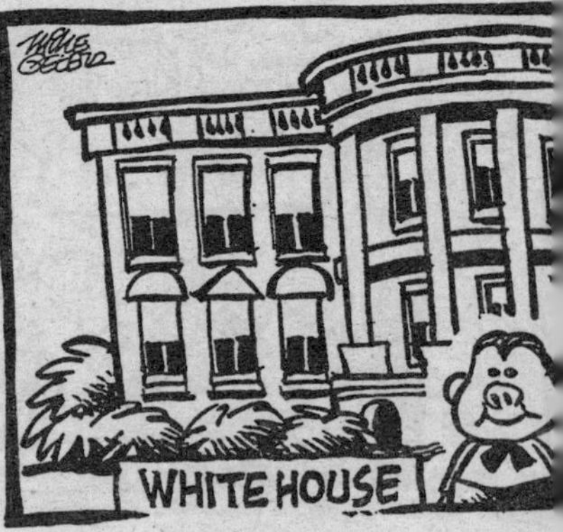
WHITE HOUSE

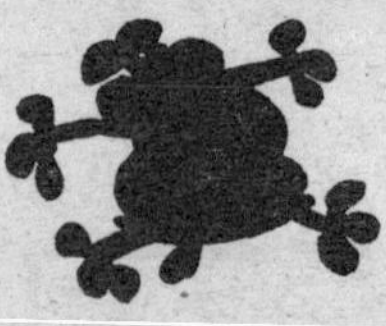

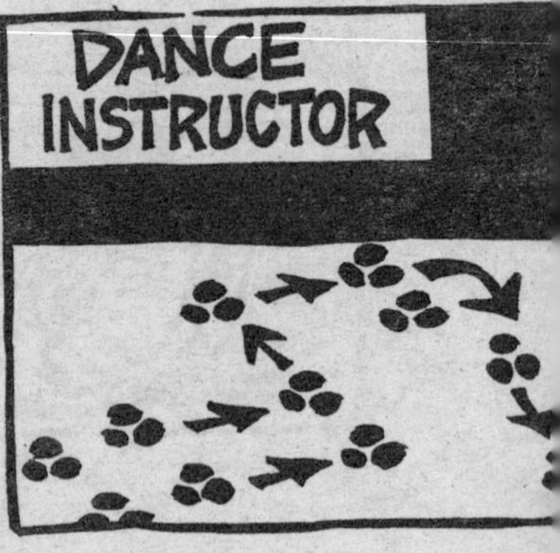
DANCE
INSTRUCTOR

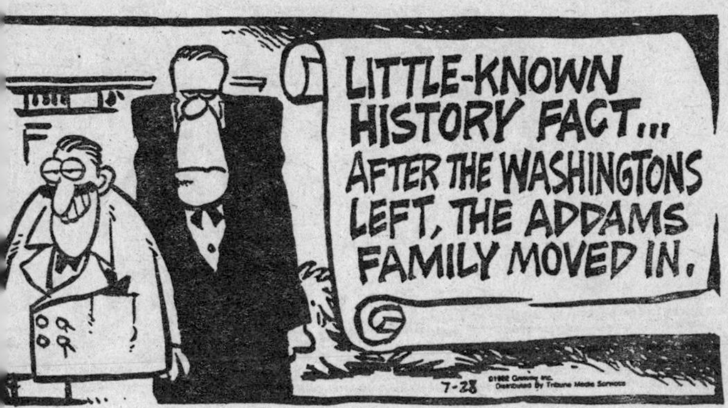
LITTLE-KNOWN HISTORY FACT... AFTER THE WASHINGTONS LEFT, THE ADDAMS FAMILY MOVED IN.
7-28
©1992 Grimmy Inc. Distributed by Tribune Media Services

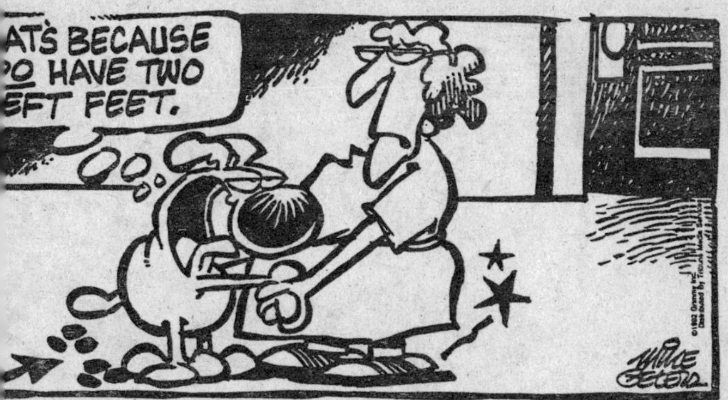
AT'S BECAUSE
DO HAVE TWO
EFT FEET.

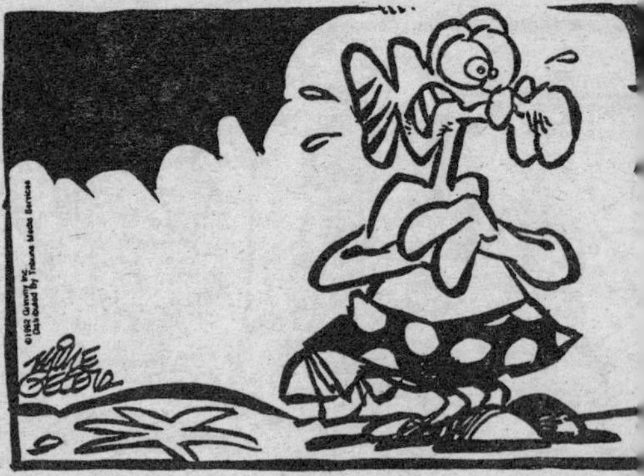
©1992 Grimmy Inc.
Distributed By Tribune Media Services

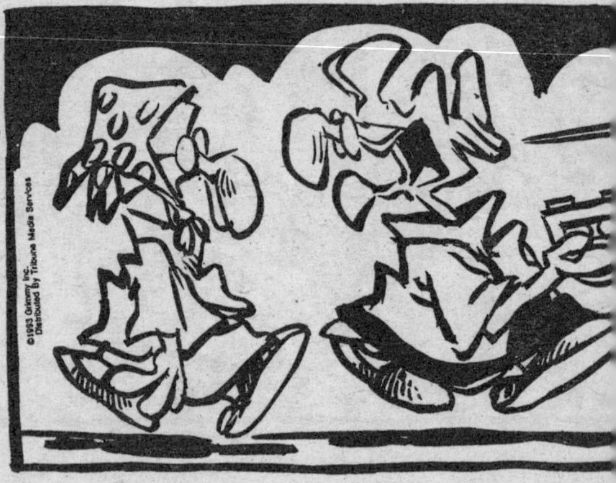
©1993 Grimmy Inc.
Distributed By Tribune Media Services

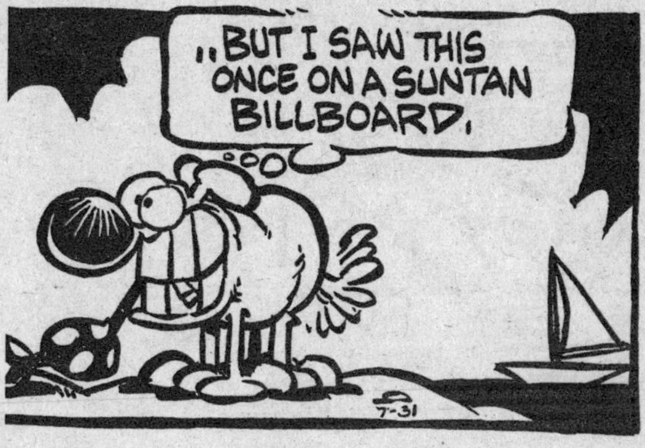
..BUT I SAW THIS ONCE ON A SUNTAN BILLBOARD.
7-31

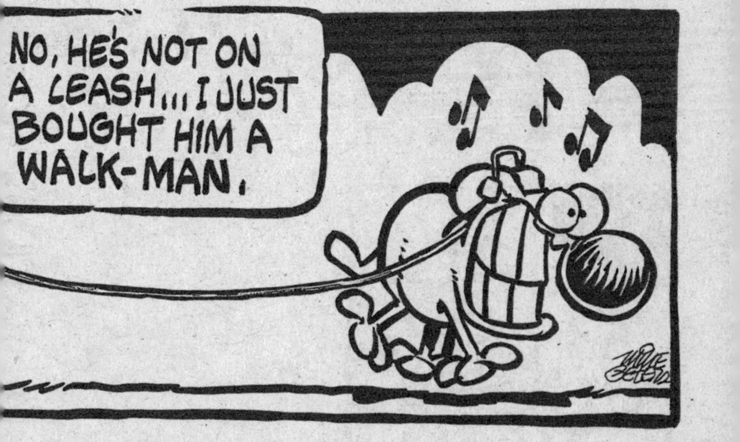
NO, HE'S NOT ON A LEASH...I JUST BOUGHT HIM A WALK-MAN.

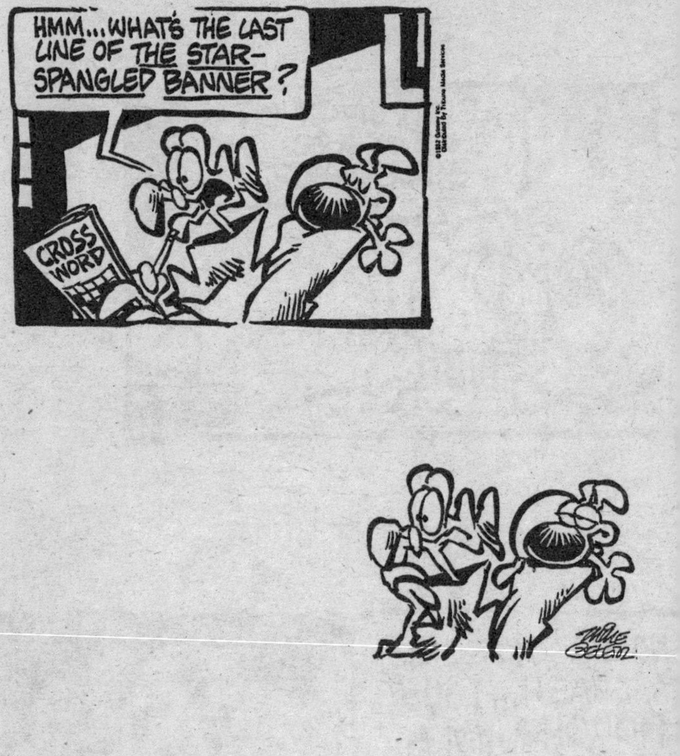
HMM...WHAT'S THE LAST LINE OF THE STAR-SPANGLED BANNER?
CROSS WORD
PLAY BALL!

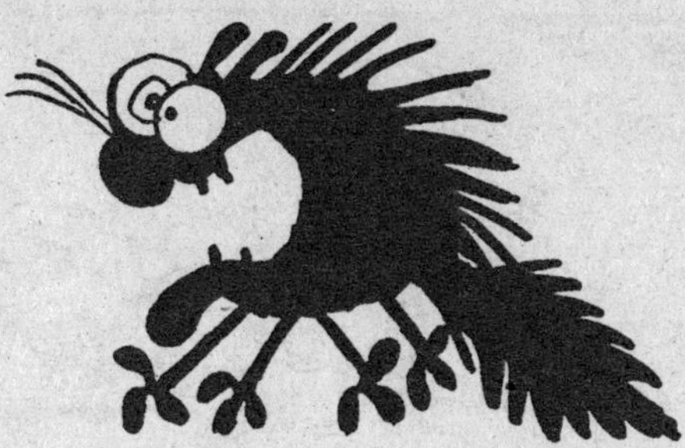

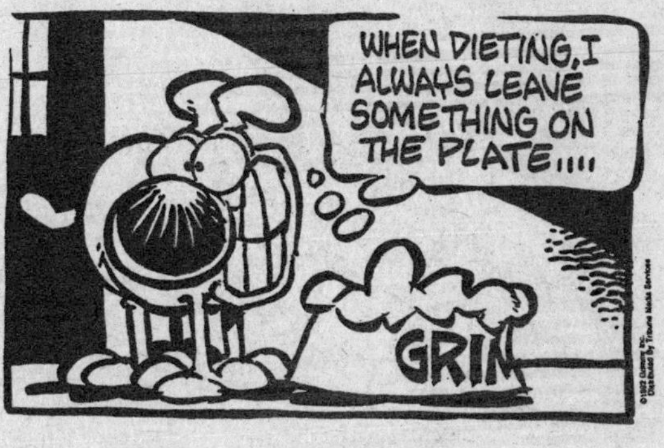
WHEN DIETING, I ALWAYS LEAVE SOMETHING ON THE PLATE....
GRIN

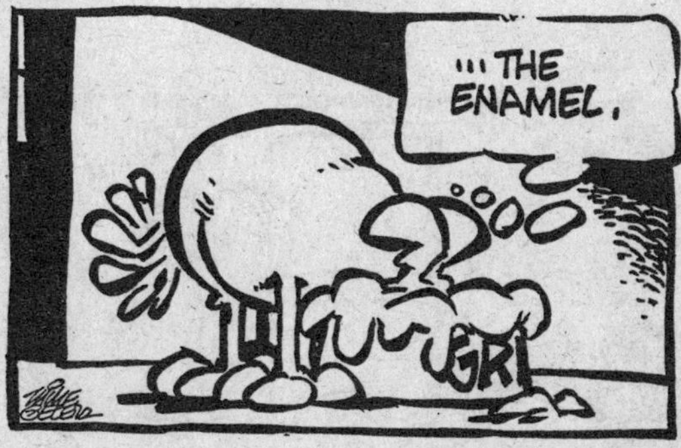
...THE ENAMEL.
GRI

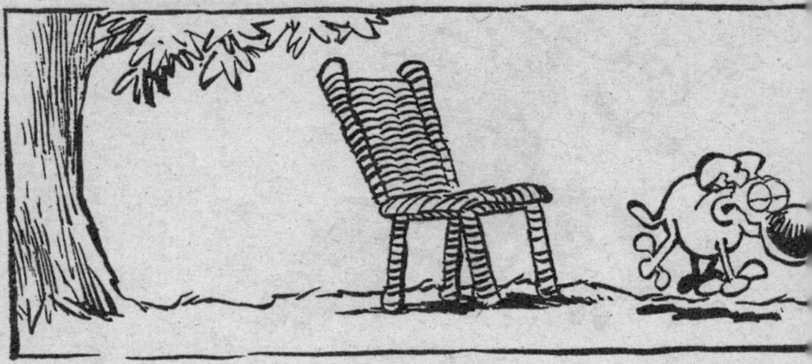

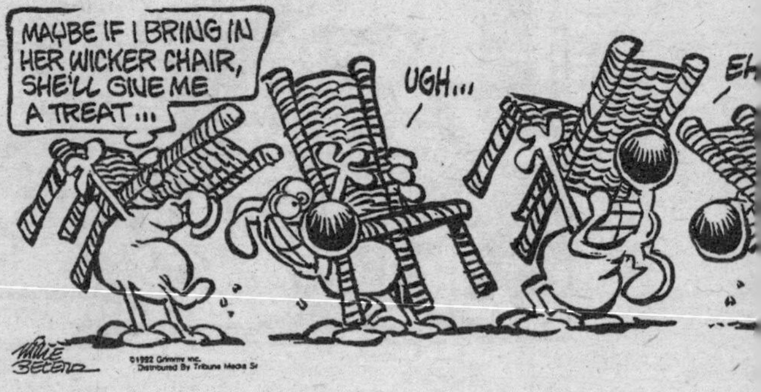
MAYBE IF I BRING IN HER WICKER CHAIR, SHE'LL GIVE ME A TREAT...
UGH...

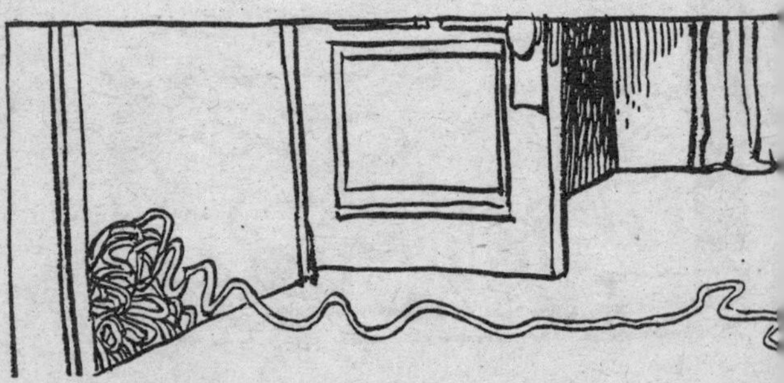

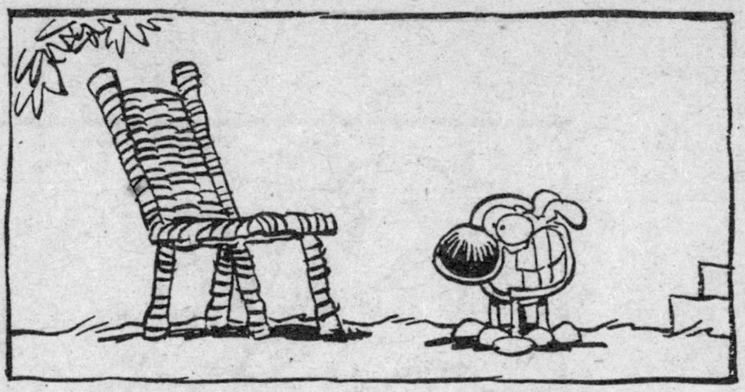

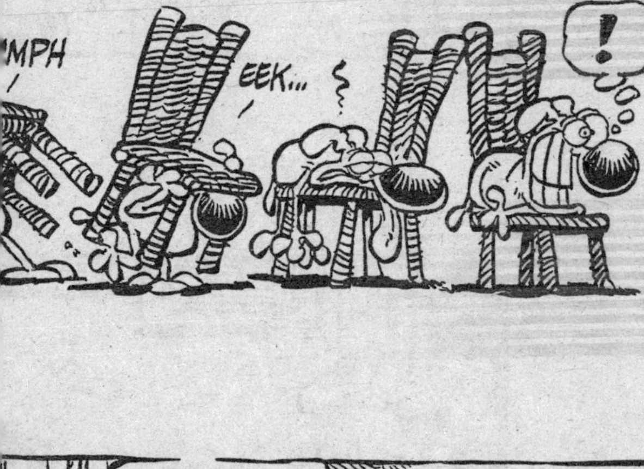
MPH
EEK...
!

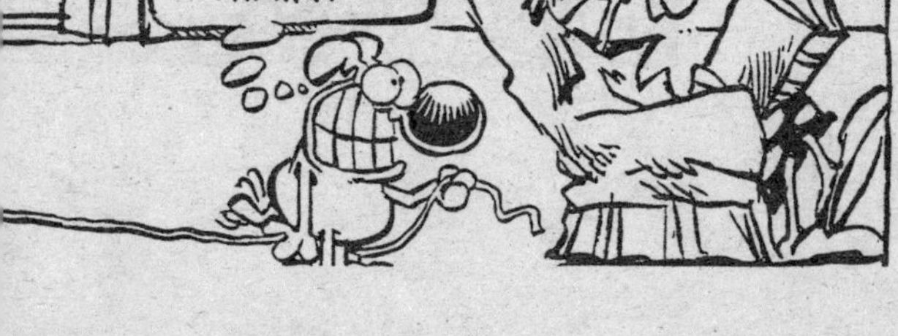
I BROUGHT IN YOUR WICKER CHAIR.

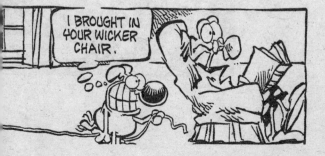

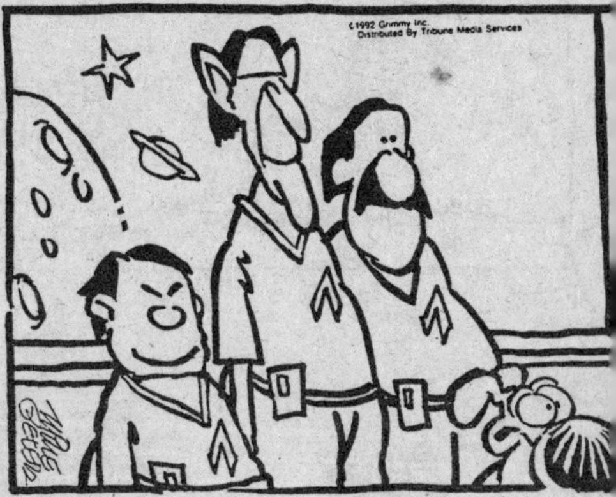
©1992 Grimmy Inc.
Distributed By Tribune Media Services

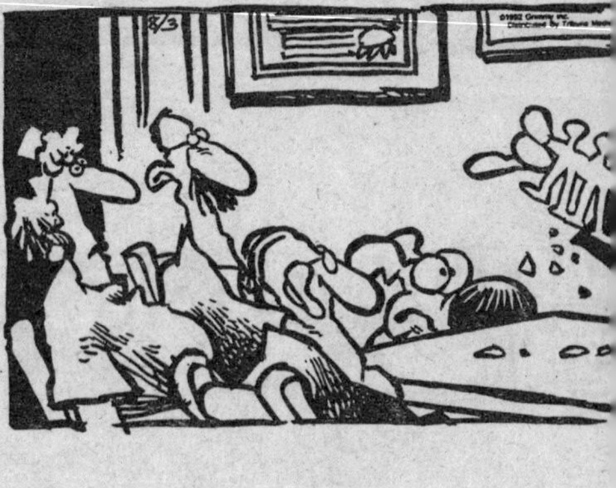
8/3
©1992 Grimmy Inc.

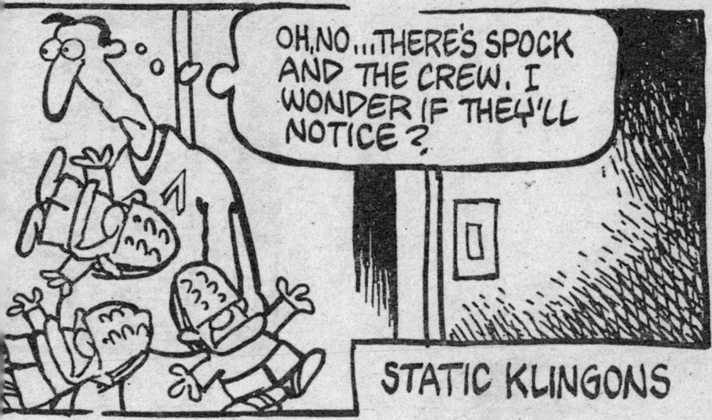
OH, NO... THERE'S SPOCK AND THE CREW. I WONDER IF THEY'LL NOTICE?

STATIC KLINGONS

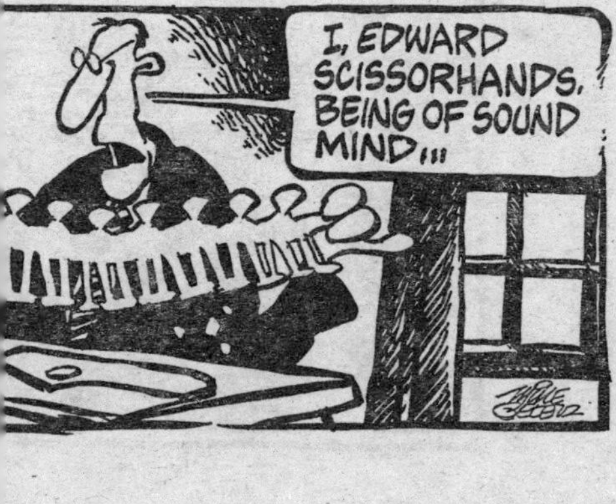
I, EDWARD SCISSORHANDS, BEING OF SOUND MIND...

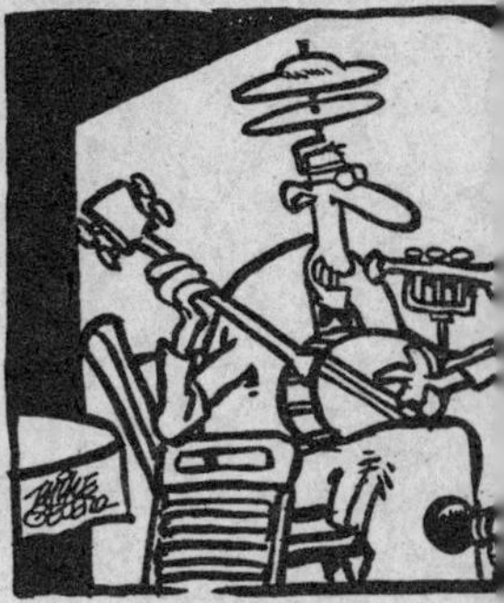

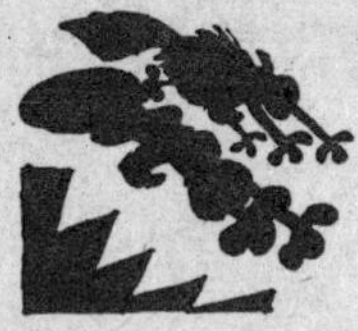

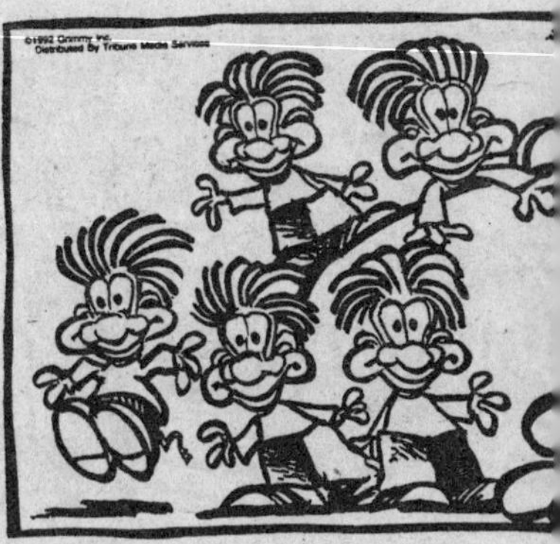

©1992 Grimmy Inc.
Distributed By Tribune Media Services

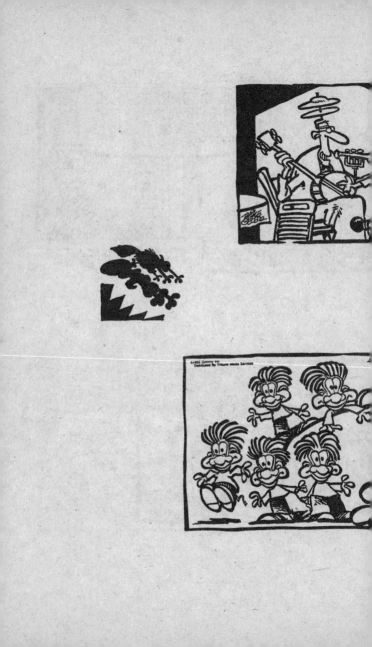

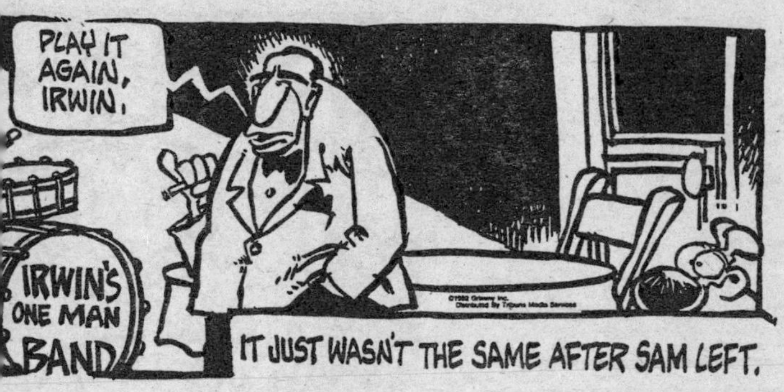
PLAY IT AGAIN, IRWIN.
IRWIN'S ONE MAN BAND
IT JUST WASN'T THE SAME AFTER SAM LEFT.

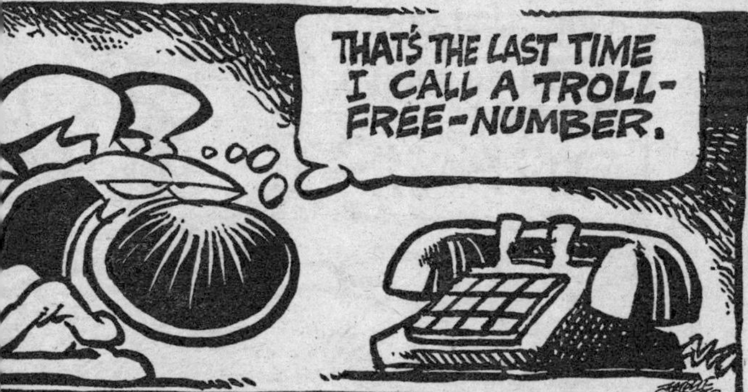
THAT'S THE LAST TIME I CALL A TROLL-FREE-NUMBER.

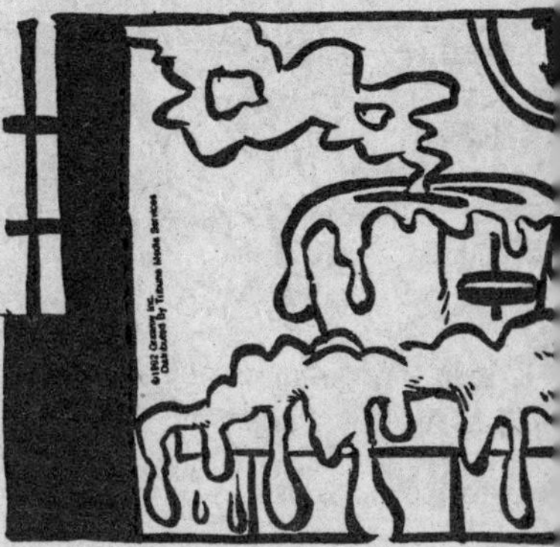

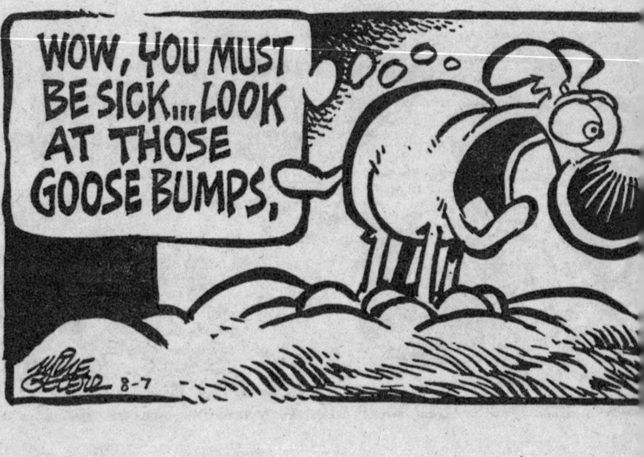
WOW, YOU MUST BE SICK... LOOK AT THOSE GOOSE BUMPS,
8-7

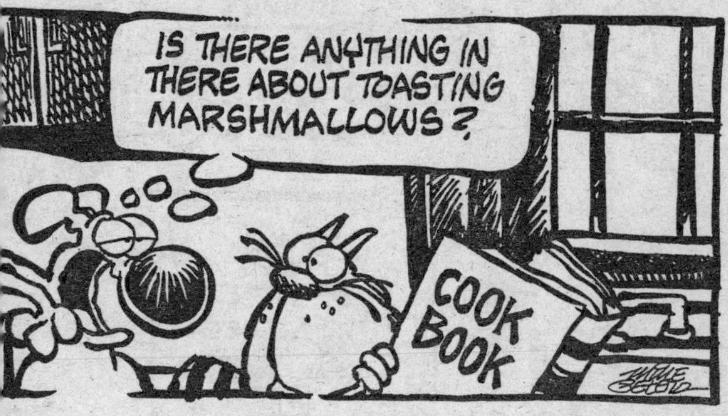
IS THERE ANYTHING IN THERE ABOUT TOASTING MARSHMALLOWS?
COOK BOOK

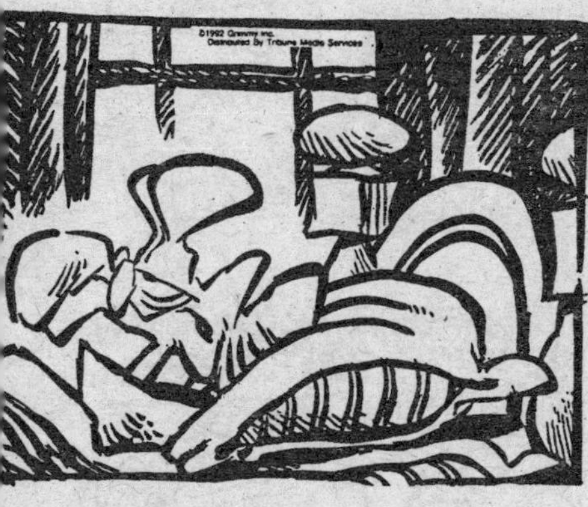
©1992 Grimmy Inc.
Distributed By Tribune Media Services

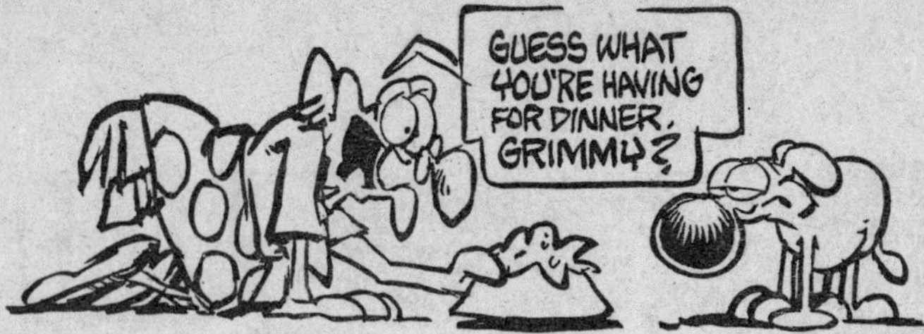
GUESS WHAT YOU'RE HAVING FOR DINNER, GRIMMY?

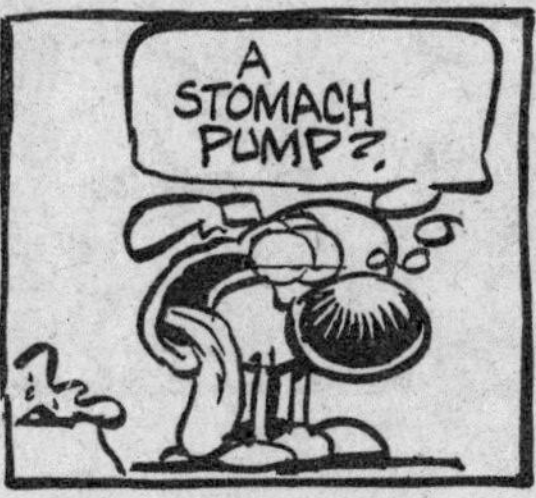
A STOMACH PUMP?

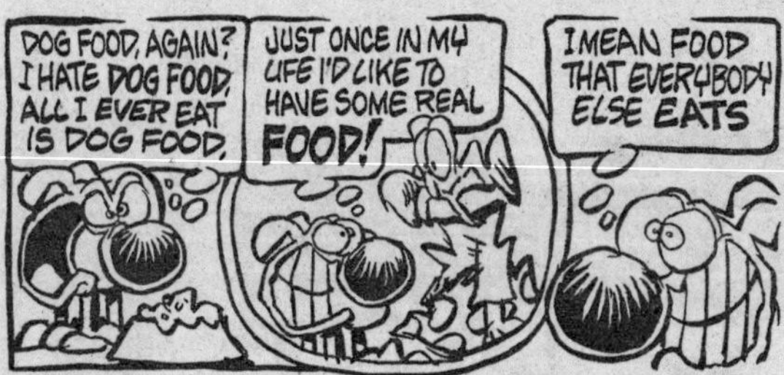
DOG FOOD, AGAIN? I HATE DOG FOOD, ALL I EVER EAT IS DOG FOOD.
JUST ONCE IN MY LIFE I'D LIKE TO HAVE SOME REAL FOOD!
I MEAN FOOD THAT EVERYBODY ELSE EATS

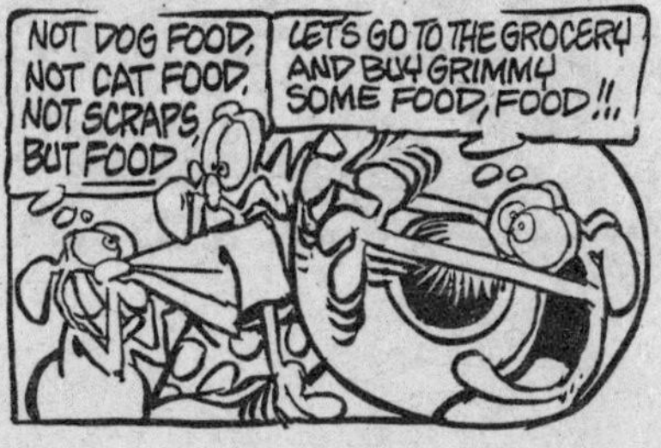
NOT DOG FOOD, NOT CAT FOOD, NOT SCRAPS, BUT FOOD
LET'S GO TO THE GROCERY AND BUY GRIMMY SOME FOOD, FOOD!!

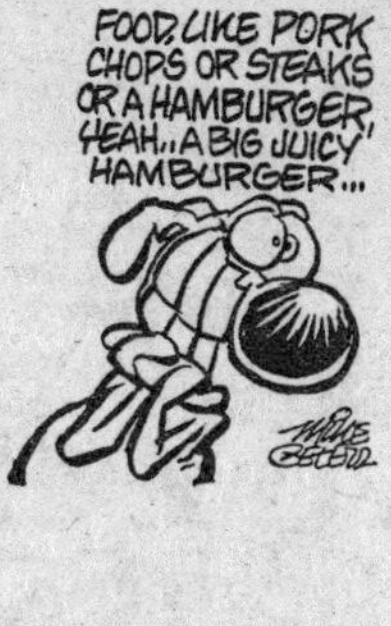
FOOD, LIKE PORK CHOPS OR STEAKS OR A HAMBURGER, YEAH.. A BIG JUICY HAMBURGER...
MIKE PETERS

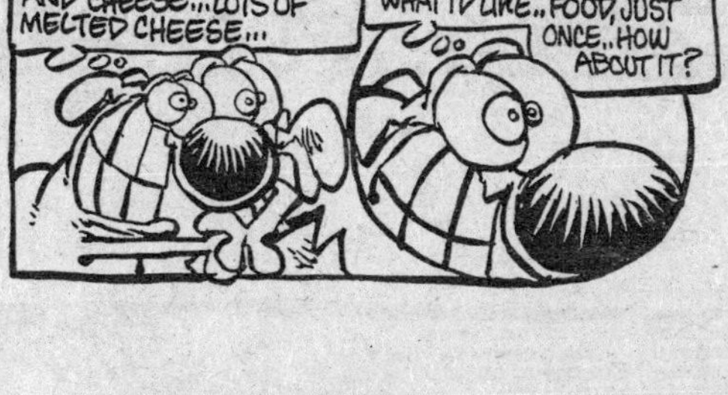
WITH LETTUCE AND ONIONS AND PICKLES AND TOMATOES AND CHEESE... LOTS OF MELTED CHEESE...
ON A TOASTED SESAME SEED BUN, YEAH, THAT'S WHAT I'D LIKE.. FOOD, JUST ONCE.. HOW ABOUT IT?

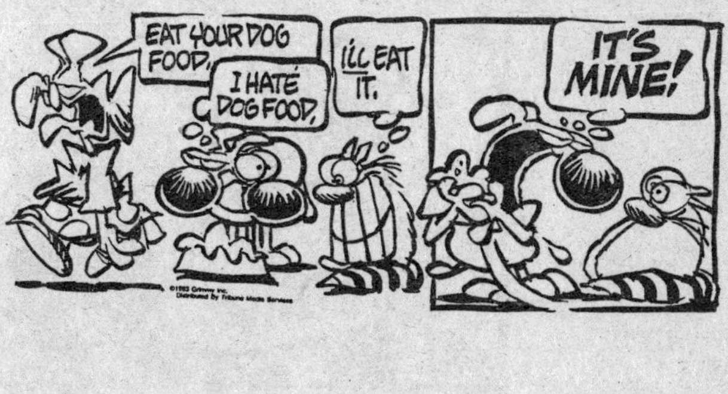
EAT YOUR DOG FOOD,
I HATE DOG FOOD,
I'LL EAT IT.
IT'S MINE!
©1983 Grimmy Inc.
Distributed by Tribune Media Services

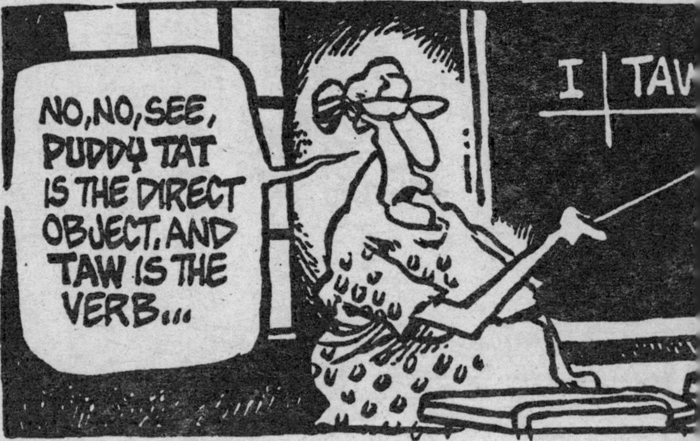
NO, NO, SEE, PUDDY TAT IS THE DIRECT OBJECT, AND TAW IS THE VERB...
I | TAW

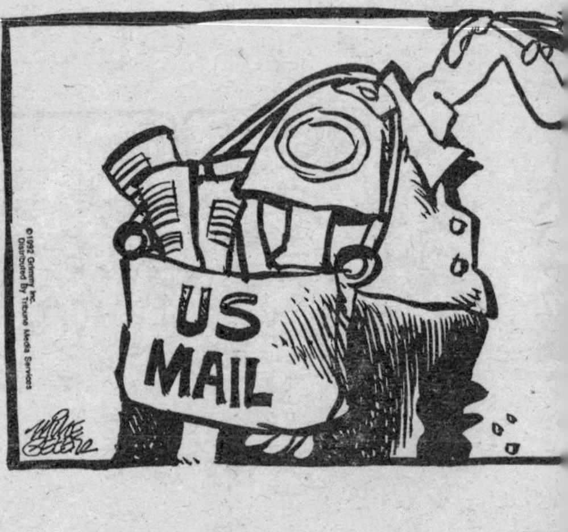
US MAIL
©1992 Grimmy, Inc. Distributed By Tribune Media Services

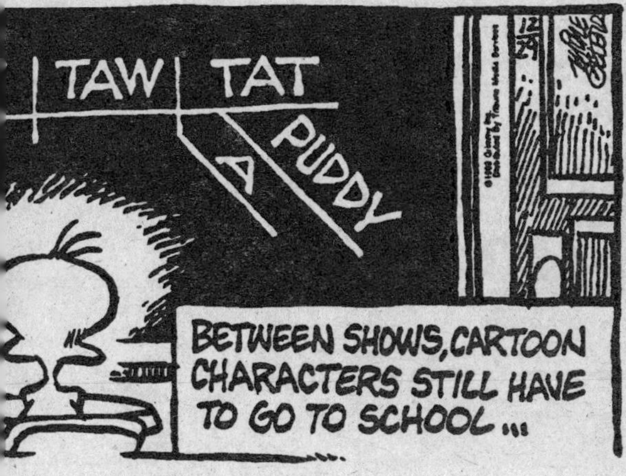
TAW TAT
A PUDDY
BETWEEN SHOWS, CARTOON CHARACTERS STILL HAVE TO GO TO SCHOOL...

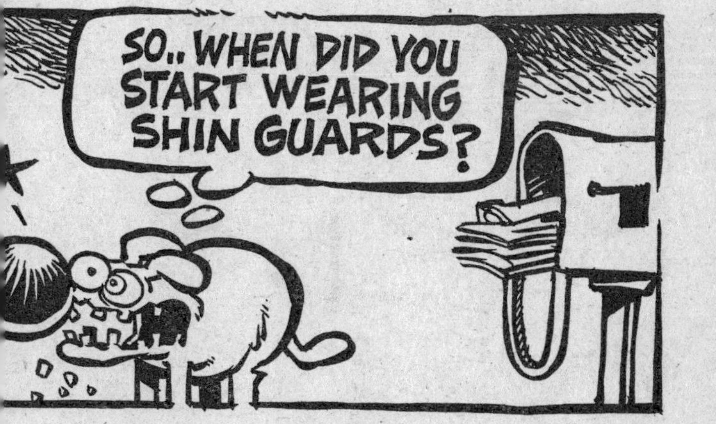
SO.. WHEN DID YOU START WEARING SHIN GUARDS?

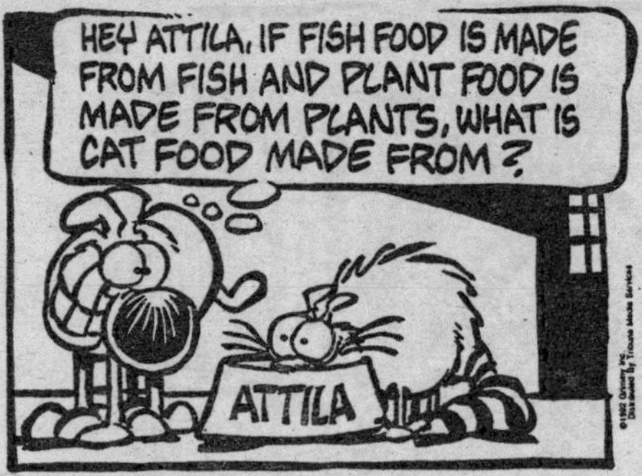
HEY ATTILA, IF FISH FOOD IS MADE FROM FISH AND PLANT FOOD IS MADE FROM PLANTS, WHAT IS CAT FOOD MADE FROM?
ATTILA
©1992 Grimmy Inc.
Distributed By Tribune Media Services

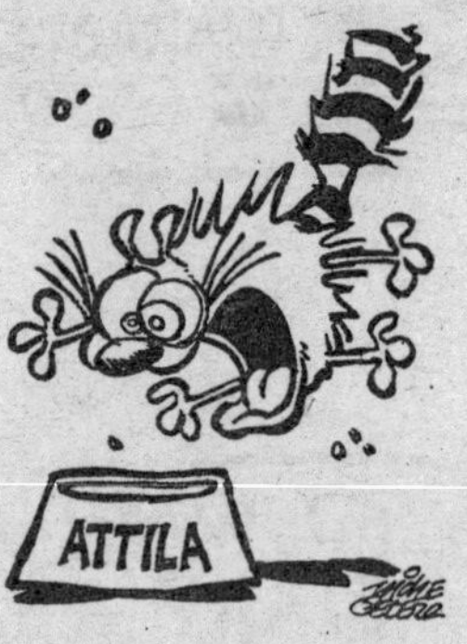
ATTILA

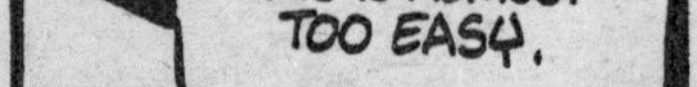
THIS IS ALMOST TOO EASY.
ATTILA

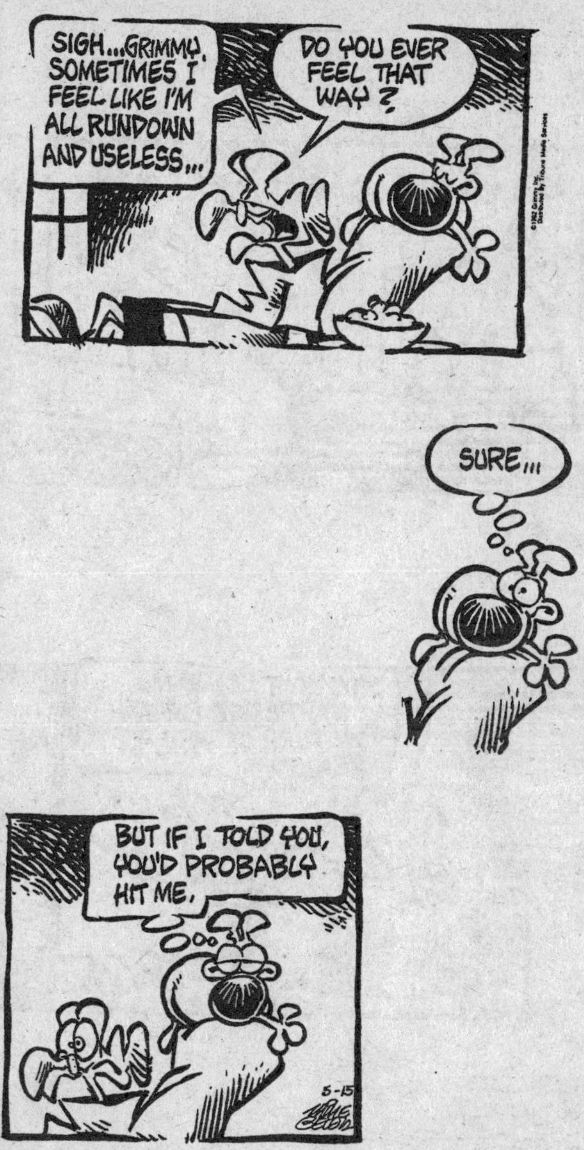
SIGH...GRIMMY, SOMETIMES I FEEL LIKE I'M ALL RUNDOWN AND USELESS...
DO YOU EVER FEEL THAT WAY?
©1992 Grimmy, Inc.
Distributed by Tribune Media Services
SURE...
BUT IF I TOLD YOU, YOU'D PROBABLY HIT ME.
5-15

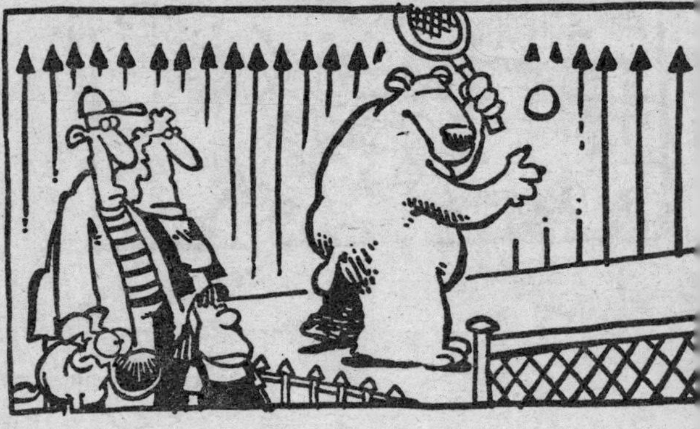

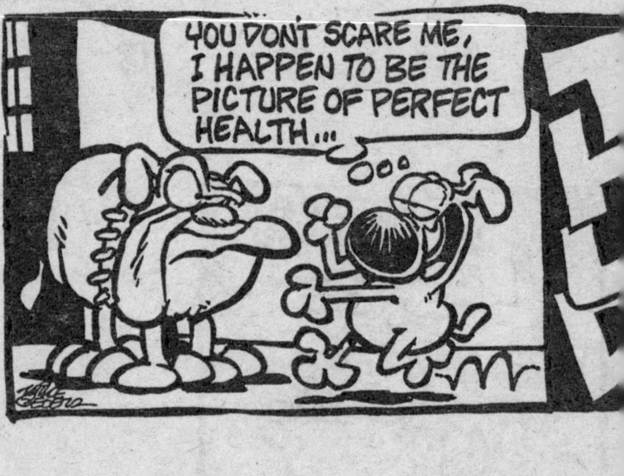
YOU DON'T SCARE ME, I HAPPEN TO BE THE PICTURE OF PERFECT HEALTH...

MINIMUM SECURITY ZOO

...ALTHOUGH THE FRAME COULD USE A LITTLE ADJUSTMENT.

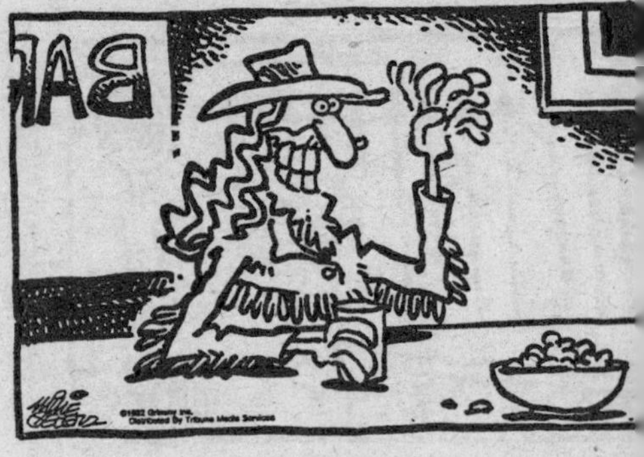

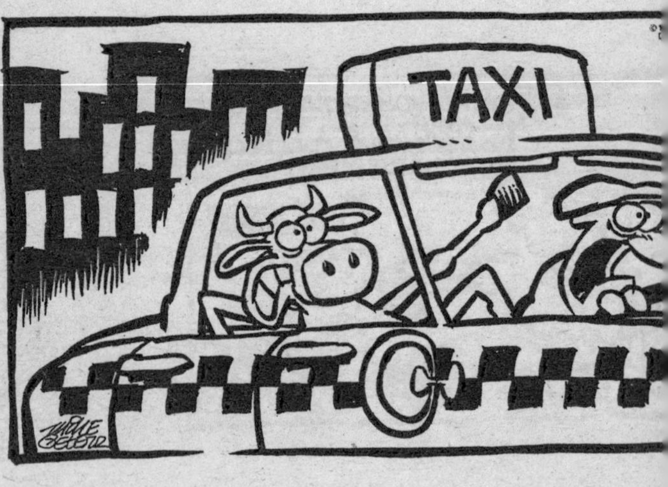
TAXI

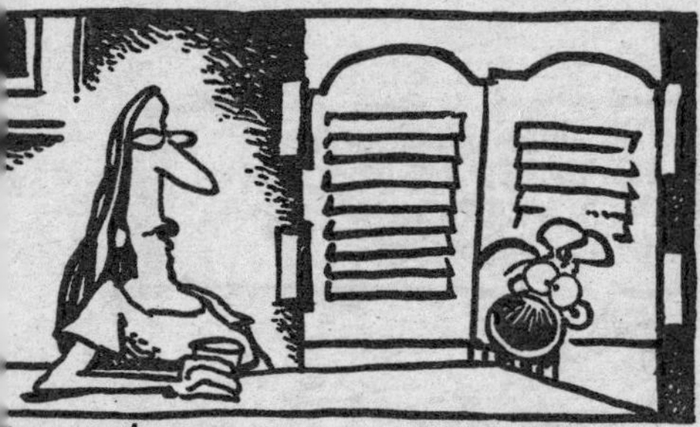

CUSTER'S LAST ONE-NIGHT STAND

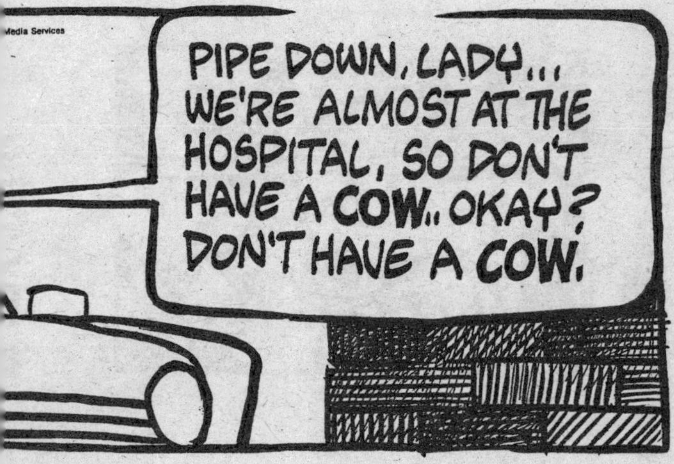
Media Services
PIPE DOWN, LADY... WE'RE ALMOST AT THE HOSPITAL, SO DON'T HAVE A COW.. OKAY? DON'T HAVE A COW.

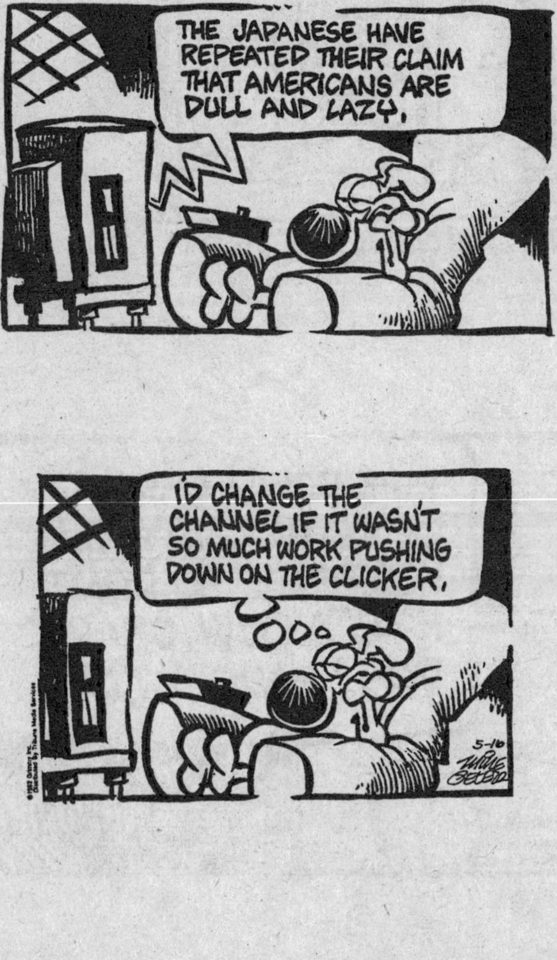
THE JAPANESE HAVE REPEATED THEIR CLAIM THAT AMERICANS ARE DULL AND LAZY.
I'D CHANGE THE CHANNEL IF IT WASN'T SO MUCH WORK PUSHING DOWN ON THE CLICKER.
5-16

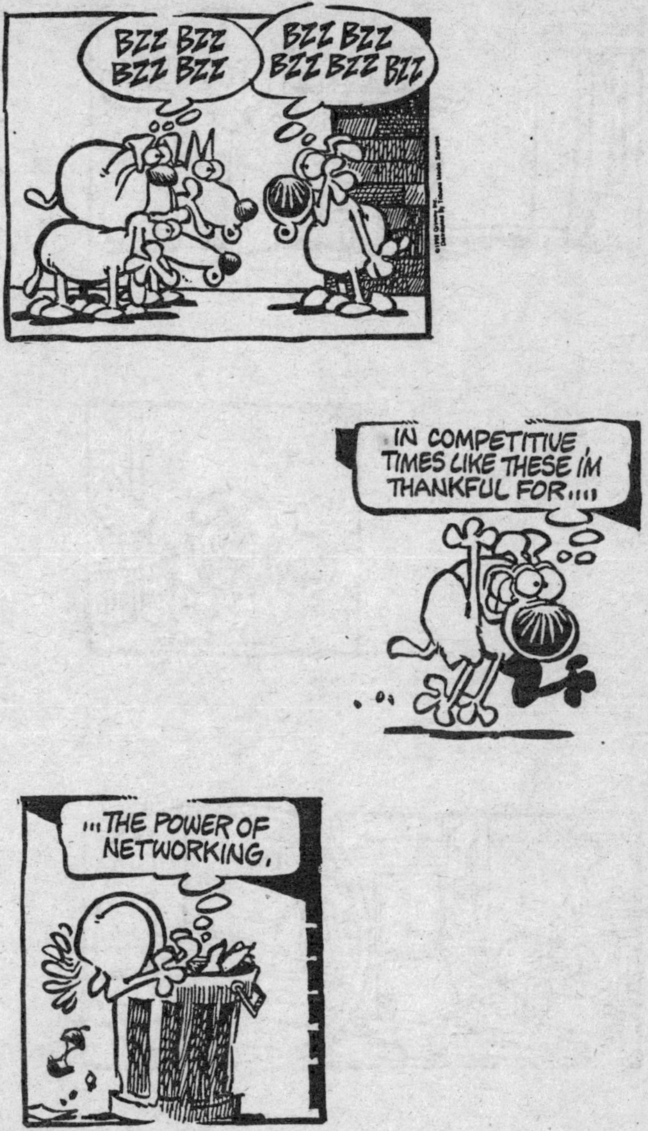
BZZ BZZ
BZZ BZZ
BZZ BZZ
BZZ BZZ BZZ
IN COMPETITIVE, TIMES LIKE THESE I'M THANKFUL FOR...
...THE POWER OF NETWORKING.

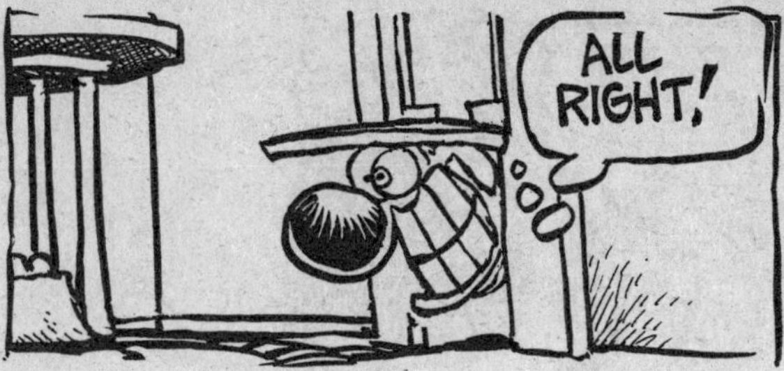
ALL RIGHT!

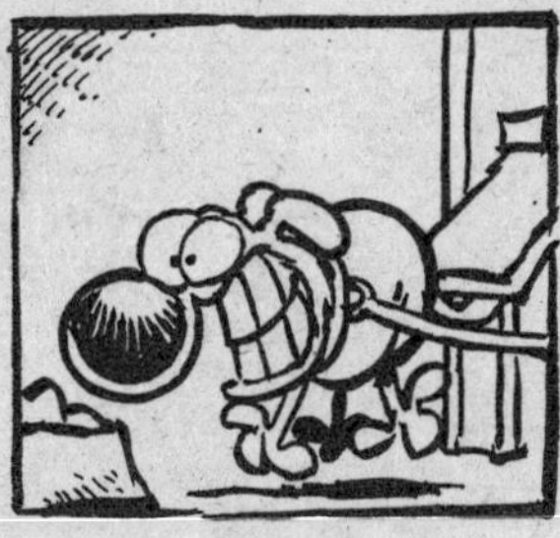

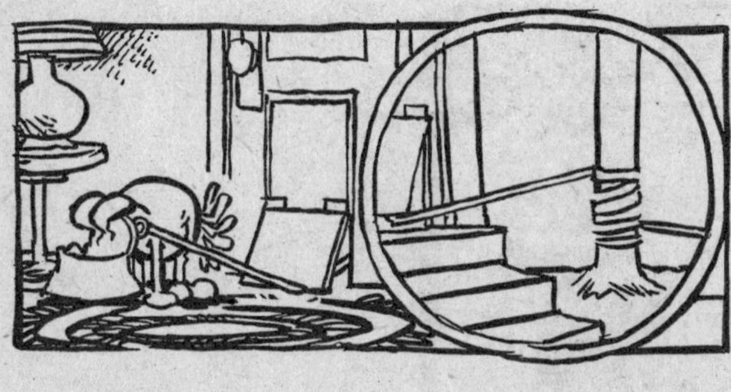

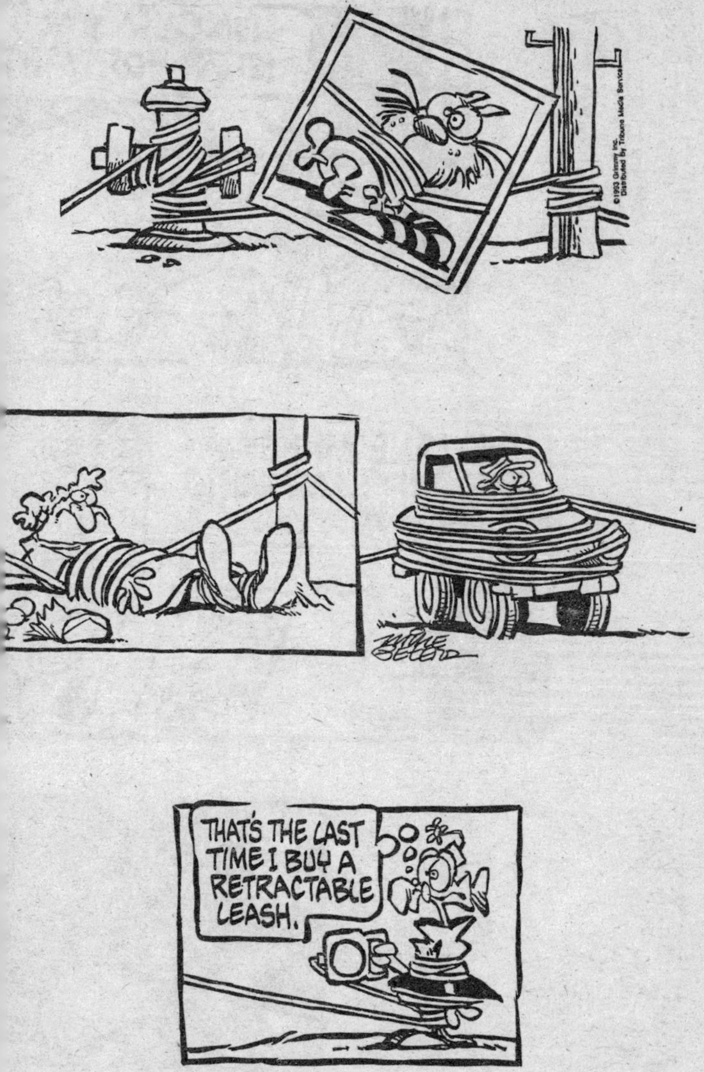
©1993 Grimmy Inc.
Distributed by Tribune Media Services
THAT'S THE LAST TIME I BUY A RETRACTABLE LEASH.

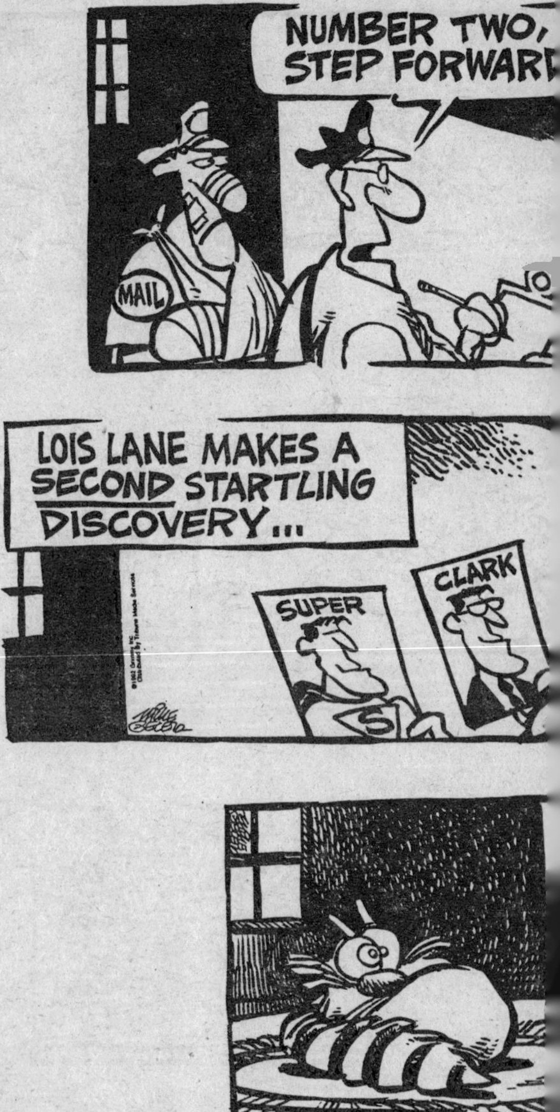
NUMBER TWO, STEP FORWAR
MAIL
LOIS LANE MAKES A SECOND STARTLING DISCOVERY...
SUPER
CLARK

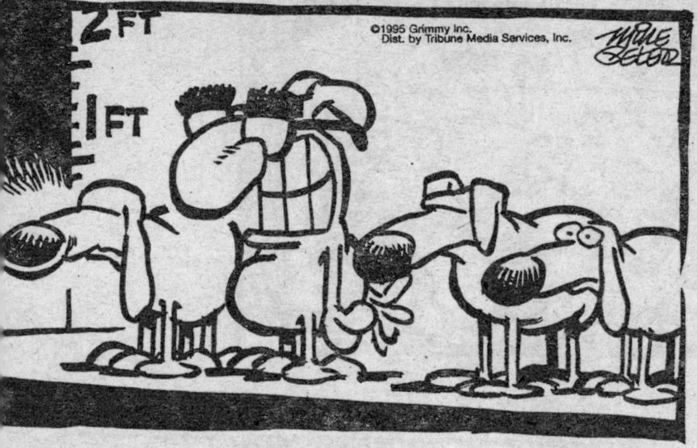
2 FT
1 FT
©1995 Grimmy Inc.
Dist. by Tribune Media Services, Inc.

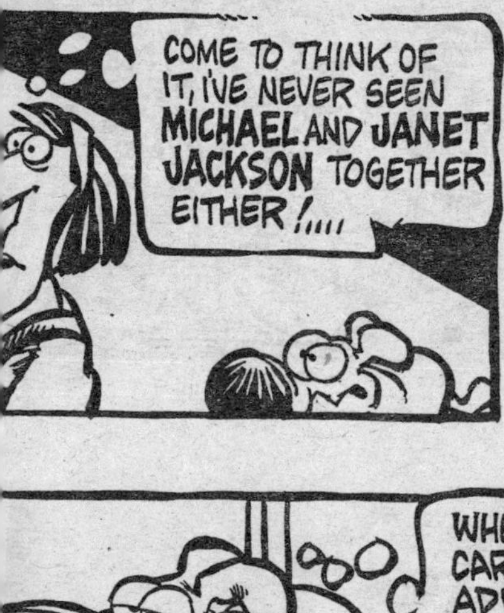
COME TO THINK OF IT, I'VE NEVER SEEN MICHAEL AND JANET JACKSON TOGETHER EITHER!....

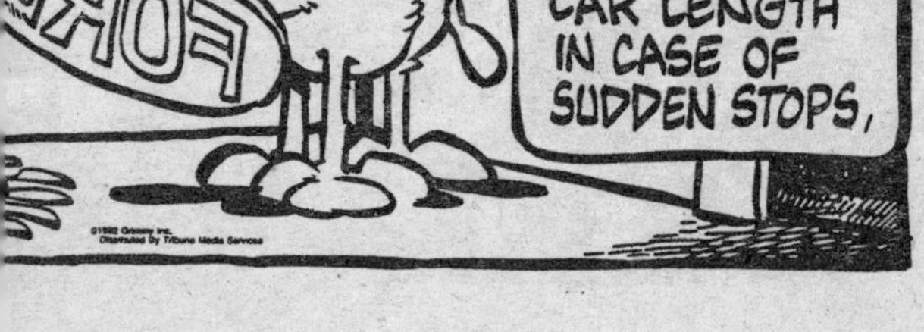
FORD
WHEN CHASING A CAR, IT'S ALWAYS ADVISABLE TO LEAVE ONE CAR LENGTH IN CASE OF SUDDEN STOPS.

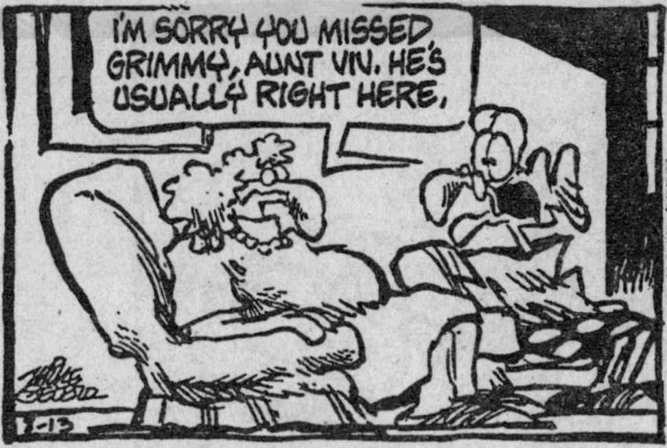
I'M SORRY YOU MISSED GRIMMY, AUNT VIV. HE'S USUALLY RIGHT HERE.

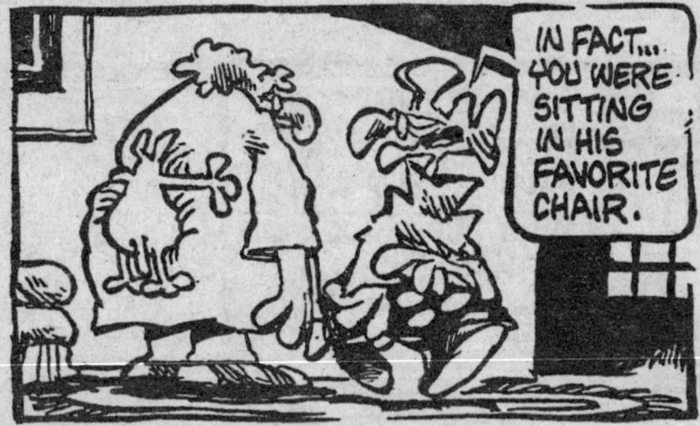
IN FACT... YOU WERE SITTING IN HIS FAVORITE CHAIR.

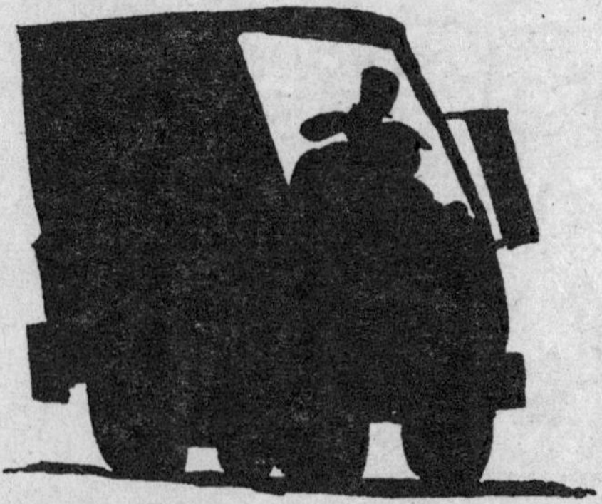

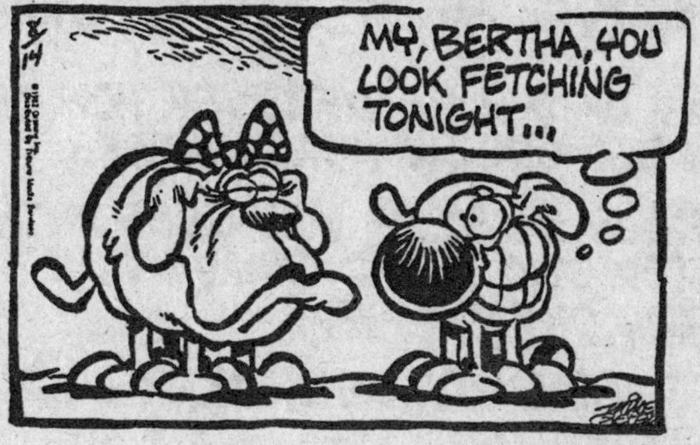
MY, BERTHA, YOU LOOK FETCHING TONIGHT...

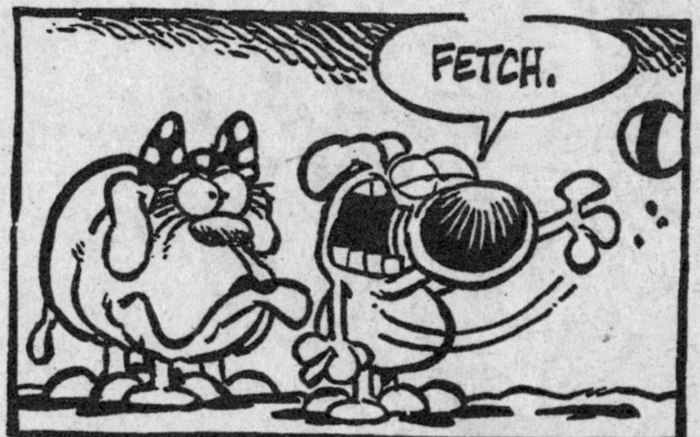
FETCH.

WHERE ARE THE GOODS?

MANY OF OUR READERS ASK HOW THEY CAN BUY GRIMMY MERCHANDISE.

HERE IS A LIST OF LICENSEES IN THE UNITED STATES AND CANADA THAT CARRY GREAT STUFF!

GIVE THEM A CALL FOR YOUR LOCAL DISTRIBUTOR.

HTTP://WWW.GRIMMY.COM

The Antioch Company 888 Dayton St. Yellow Springs, OH 45387	PH 800/543-2397 Bookmarks, Wallet Cards, **"Largely Literary"** products: T-Shirts, Mugs, Journals, Pens, Notepads, Bookplates, Bookmarks
Avalanche Publishing 1093 Bedman St. Carson, CA 90746	PH 310/223-1600 365 Day Box Calendar-Year 2000
Classcom, Inc. 770 Bertrand Montreal, Quebec Canada H4M1V9	PH 514/747-9492 Desk Art
C.T.I. 22160 North Pepper Rd. Barrington, IL 60010	PH 800/284-5605 Balloons, Coffee Mugs
F.X. Schmid/USA 11 Industrial Way Salem, NH 03079	PH 800/886-1236 Puzzles
Gibson Greetings 2100 Section Rd. Cincinnati, OH 45237	PH 800/345-6521 Greeting Cards, Party Papers, Gift Wrap etc... www.greetst.com
Linda Jones Enterprises 17771 Mitchell Irvine, CA 92614	PH 714/660-7791 Cels
MR. Tees 3225 Hartsfield Rd. Tallahassee, FL 32303	PH 850/574-3737 T-Shirts
Pomegranate 210 Classic Ct. Rohnert Park, CA 94928	PH 800/227-1428 Wall Year 2000 Calendars, Postcard Booklets
Put Me On, Inc. 623 - 29th St. South Birmingham, AL 35233	PH 800/466-8823 T-Shirts www.putmeontshirts.com
Second Nature Software 1325 Officers' Row Vancouver, WA 98661	PH 360/737-4170 Screen Saver Program www.secondnature.com
TOR Books 175 Fifth Ave. New York, NY 10010	PH 212/388-0100 Paperback Books